Dare To Ask God WHY?

GREG WILLIAMS

TREATY OAK PUBLISHERS

Publisher's Note

Dare to Ask God Why? is a work of inspiration and individual memoir. All of the characters, business establishments, and events are based on the author's personal experiences. Some individuals' names have been changed to protect their privacy. Scripture references unless otherwise noted are taken from the *New International Version* and the *New Living Translation* in the public domain.

Copyright © 2018 by Greg Williams

Cover design by Kimberly Greyer
All rights reserved.

No part of this book may be reproduced, scanned, or distributed in any printed or electronic form without permission from the author. Please do not participate in or encourage piracy of copyrighted materials in violation of the author's rights. Purchase only authorized editions.

**Printed and published
in the United States of America**

Treaty Oak Publishers

ISBN-13: 978-1-943658-30-5

DEDICATION

To the two who gave me life, Nelson & Annie,
and the one who gives my life purpose, Nic

TABLE OF CONTENTS

INTRODUCTION		1
CHAPTER 1:	"Dissats"	11
CHAPTER 2:	The Call	19
CHAPTER 3:	Day 1	31
CHAPTER 4:	Day 2 (A.M.)	55
CHAPTER 5:	Day 2 (P.M.)	91
CHAPTER 6:	Day 3	111
CHAPTER 7:	Day 4	139
CHAPTER 8:	The Choice	153
CHAPTER 9:	Reconciliation	165
CHAPTER 10:	Home Going	179
CHAPTER 11:	Battle	195
CHAPTER 12:	Promise	207
CHAPTER 13:	The Midas Touch	237
CHAPTER 14:	So	263
Appendix		277
ACKNOWLEDGEMENTS		291

Dare To Ask God WHY?

GREG WILLIAMS

INTRODUCTION

It's inevitable. Every human being, regardless of their faith, belief, or religion, will at some point witness or experience a tragedy of life. For many, their responses will often lead to a question regarding God's lack of intervention.

As a believer, we are taught as a matter of convenience to accept the typical Christian responses:

"It's God's will."

"It's part of God's plan."

or simply

"Trust God."

These clichés do very little in offering solace to personal tragedy and often leave you feeling abandoned by God. This book offers an example to help understand and respond to the heartbreak by challenging the status quo. After experiencing my own trial, I too felt abandoned and the question of "Why" dogged me nonstop. Instead of succumbing to the desires of my emotions—incessant crying—I dared to ask God why, and he responded by leading me on an incredible journey of unimaginable discovery, love, and grace.

Having faith is the foundation of being a Christian. Without faith, it's impossible to maintain a meaningful relationship with God. And with it comes an assurance that God's love will sustain you throughout your life. Unfortunately, it doesn't guarantee your life will be free from trials, but with assurance in knowing that whatever challenge arises, you will emerge victorious.

THIS BOOK EXPLORES THE complexities of maintaining my faith and trusting God when my absolute worst life-changing event occurred. My son was stricken with bacterial meningitis, a highly debilitating—and sometimes deadly—disease.

My faith was shaken to its core, and at my lowest point, I even questioned God's existence. As my tragedy unfolded, I asked God a series of whys:

Why did you allow this to happen?

Why aren't my prayers being answered?

Why did you abandon me?

And why should I trust you?

The following chapters are actual events that occurred surrounding my son's illness and my interpretation of those events.

☆ ☆ ☆

THE WILLIAMS

Greg (Dad):

I'm a middle-age divorcé who works as a procurement administrator for a local university. Very convincing at projecting an outgoing persona, but my self-doubts prevent me from maximizing my full potential. Once an avid tennis player, but age took its toll on my arthritic knees and sidelined me to a life as a reluctant spectator.

Being the often overlooked middle child, I have an innate desire to be recognized and affirmed. Raised by a strict disciplinarian mother and a conservative and emotionally distant father, I accept responsibility with ease, but I developed passive-aggressive tendencies. As a self-described "lukewarm Christian," I've always attended church regularly, but I lacked a personal relationship/connection with God.

My claim to fame is the relationship with my two children whom I affectionately refer to as the "monsters." Becoming a dad was the absolute most important role in my life and without a doubt, the most rewarding! The day of their births, I took a vow to become the best dad I could be. My commitment to myself and to them was that, no matter what, I would always be involved in all aspects of their lives. So determined with my commitment, I often mentioned that my obituary would simply read "Committed and Loving Father."

Arlene (Mom):

Divorced after a twenty-three-year marriage, Arlene didn't adjust well and harbors some resentment toward me for the failure of our marriage. Comfortable in a crowded room where she doesn't know a soul, she soon adjusts and becomes the "life of the party." Raised by a very dominant mother, Arlene can be highly opinionated and lacks the ability to see things from an opposing perspective. A loyal friend to the end, she expects the same commitment in return. As an accountant, she can be stubborn about anything.

Her commitment to our children equals mine,

which provided a good balance while rearing Tiffany and Nicolis. Clearly the disciplinarian of the two parents, Arlene ensured her children were well grounded in religion, education, and social skills. She's demanding but fair. Both children understood their mom would move heaven and hell for their benefit.

Tiffany, (Tootie), (Monster):

Is similar to a wildflower blowing in the wind without a care in the world. Her "easy come, easy go" approach to life can be without doubt attributed to being the first born and first grandchild on my side of the family. By receiving tons of attention during her developing years, she grew up believing that fate would provide all the necessities of life. At the time of her brother's illness, she was a senior at the University of Texas at San Antonio, majoring in history. Like all proud first-time parents, I believed Tiffany was God's greatest creation and she was the most beautiful bundle of joy I'd ever laid eyes on.

Because of Tiffany, I understood the lifelong commitment and special bond between fathers and daughters. Even after her marriage and then having her own family, I believe I will always have a role in her life. Daughters will always be dad's "little girl," and in return we hope they view us as their knights in shining armor. Tiffany is the ultimate optimist and sees only the positives in everyone. Her philosophy is, all we need is love and the rest will take care of itself.

Nicolis, (Nic), (Monster), (Nico):

Nic, the nickname for Nicolis, was quite a gregarious and sensitive child. Early on, he exhibited a very strong desire to be around people. He hated being alone and was willing to do almost anything to avoid the loneliness of isolation. Nic is the only grandson on my side of the family and, as expected, my father took a very distinct interest in him. As Nic's grandfather neared the last days of his life, he thought more and more about his legacy and Nic represented that. My father was thrilled that his branch of the Williams' family tree would continue for at least another generation.

As Nic grew older, his desire to be accepted caused severe problems. During his freshman year in high school, his African-American friends viewed him as being too "white" and his white friends thought he wasn't "black" enough. Needless to say, he had a difficult time adjusting. At times he cried and pleaded, "What's wrong with me? Why can't I make friends? Why do they make fun of me?" We encouraged Nic by telling him nothing was wrong and he would eventually find his niche. We advised him to give it time, don't try so hard, and sooner or later things will change.

As he approached his senior year in high school, he found that niche and we noticed a change in his personality. New friends hung around at the house like never before, and he hung out at their houses as well. He went to parties and football games, doing all the crazy things teenagers do. He at last achieved what he desperately longed for for so many years: acceptance by his peers. No longer was he not black enough or too white. He was simply Nic and a good friend to be around.

After high school graduation, Nic applied at several universities, but his heart was set on attending Texas A&M University. He wanted to be an Aggie more than anything. At first I wasn't sold on A&M, but if they offered him a scholarship, I would have stuck an "Aggie's Dad" bumper sticker on my car with pride.

About three weeks before school started, Nic received the news he dreamed of. He was accepted at the highly prominent Texas A&M University. From that day on, it was as if heaven had opened its doors and his life would never be the same. Because his acceptance was so late, all university dorm rooms were occupied and he was forced to live in an off-campus apartment. Although overjoyed with the news, we preferred an on-campus dorm room, hoping he would experience an authentic freshman lifestyle his first year.

Nic was keenly aware of everything we gave

over the years to prepare him for his new journey and he was genuinely thankful. His sensitivity, his consideration for others, and his ability to convey that sincerity were attributes his family and friends most admired about him. As a junior majoring in economics, he looked forward to attending law school after graduation.

CHAPTER 1

"DISSATS"

Blessed is the one who reads aloud the words of this prophecy, and blessed are those who hear it and take to heart what is written in it, because the time is near.
Revelations 1:3 (NIV)

For some of us, there are times in our lives when we're given insight about a future event, yet because of "dissats," we can't hear or see the obvious clues. As a society, the vast majority of us awake each morning, check our cell phone, turn on a radio or television, and begin our day receiving a constant barrage of endless, mindless chatter to which I refer as "dissats."

The term is my abbreviation for "distractions by Satan."

Dissats prevent us from experiencing what's really going on all around us and divert our attention to a consciousness manipulated by consumerism, instant gratification, selfishness and greed. All day every day we're bombarded with advertisements hoping to influence our buying patterns. Marketers use algorithms to manipulate consumers with no end in sight. On the way to our jobs, it's almost impossible to ignore the endless advertising messages, while their sole purpose is to grab our attention for that critical second or two. And, when we do arrive at work, the Internet and its pop-up ads are waiting and competing for our attention as well. During the time we're supposed to be working, we spend endless hours texting, updating social media, and following the latest topics involving celebrities, sports, relationships, sales, sex, religion, politics... and the list goes on and on.

Dissats, dissats, and more dissats.

We return home after a long day's work and start our second shift, which could be a part-time job or studying for hours into the night. If we're lucky enough to have a family, we could face homework to assist, dinner to make, clothes to prepare, kitchen to clean, checking in on a parent, paying bills, walking the dog, finding time for your spouse... and again, the list goes on and on.

Before we fall asleep, we get sucker-punched once more with a final blow of dissats. Many of us will watch our favorite television show or catch up on the latest news reports before we call it a night. Whether the program is a sitcom, a reality show, a drama, a sports event, or even an educational program, they're all designed to seize our attention and maintain it until the advertisers make an impermeable imprint in our brains.

"Dissats."

At the end of a long day, their impact at last knocks us out and we hope for a good night's sleep so we can do it all over again the next day.

Is there any more reason why we can't hear God's message?

Three specific incidents were premonitions of what was about to occur, yet the dissats of my life prevented me from seeing the obvious.

☆ ☆ ☆

The first indication was a letter I wrote to Nic:

Several months before Nic's attack, I felt an incredible need to write him a letter, but at the time, I couldn't understand why. Seeing him when he returned home from college and speaking with him regularly, I had no reason to write him. As the months passed, the desire became unavoidable. On November 11th, I gave in to the constant urging and wrote the letter. By not understanding the purpose of the letter, I was clueless where to start. I began by expressing my love for Nic and went on from there. At first thinking the letter would only be a page or two, I surprised myself by writing until it ended up about twelve pages long.

The words kept coming and coming to a point where I described the document as "A Life Letter to My Son." Somehow, the letter morphed into advice on navigating life's many challenges. By sharing my life lessons and experiences, I was preparing him for a day when death robbed us of our time together. Of course, the death in question was mine.

See Appendix for the actual letter.

The second indication was a book entitled *The Shack:*

During the spring of 2010, a former coworker, Trish McDonald, invited me to attend church services at Lakewood Church. As a good friend, Trish shared with me that God had a major purpose for my life. I didn't dismiss her conviction, but I wasn't sure where that conviction originated. After a few months of attending Lakewood, Trish gave me a book to read, *The Shack* by William Paul Young. She was not sure why I should read that particular book, but she was convinced God had placed it on her heart to give it to me.

A very popular book, it was a bestseller in 2007 about a man named Mack who lost his faith in God when his daughter was brutally murdered while on a family camping trip. The book mentions a "Great Sadness," which was a very serious case of depression that overtook Mack's life after the death of his daughter. The Great Sadness paralyzed Mack socially, emotionally, and professionally, and was a key factor in the loss of his faith.

Years later, he received a mysterious invitation to this cabin deep in the woods. While there, he encountered three people whom he at first rejected: God, Jesus, and the Holy Spirit.

After being convinced of their authenticity and that he was not crazy, Mack held very intense and thought provoking conversations with the Trinity about his loss of faith, the death of his daughter, the love God has for all his children, the role of the Trinity, and forgiveness. As the story ends, the father's faith is restored and he understands that, although terrible things can occur in life, God is forever present and his unrelenting love will sustain us, if we only believe in him.

I found the book very entertaining as it explained God's purpose in our lives, but "why me?" still required an answer. Trish's only response was that God had a specific plan for my life and the book would help me with it.

Help me how?

I did not have a clue as to what she was talking about, but I found the story heartwarming to see Mack reconnect with God and regain his faith. Still, she couldn't explain it, so at some point, I put it behind me and moved on.

The third indication was a repeated message from a friend:

Sarah Hinojosa was another close friend I'd known for years and she also worked in higher education. Sarah is a very family oriented woman who's vehemently committed to her two children, Nicolas and Sandra. As the only sibling of eight in her family to achieve a college education, she expected no less from her children. Like most parents, Nicolas and Sandra meant everything to her, and she worked diligently to ensure they had all they needed to succeed in life.

During our years working together, Sarah often confided in me about a reoccurring feeling she had regarding Nicolas, the younger of her two children. They called him Nico for short, and she would often reveal a fear that he was going to die at an early age. Why would she say such a horrible thing? She endured the feeling for many years, but now it became more prevalent and she had no idea why. Because of her conviction, she vowed to spend as much time with Nico as she could.

Startled, my eyes cringed with disbelief of her revelations because no parent can ever imagine the death of their child. Psychologists agree that the death of a child is the worst experience a parent can encounter and many cannot recover from the loss.

I tried to reassure her that Nico would outlive her and she had no reason ever to feel that way. Nico was a perfectly healthy eleven-year-old with his whole long life ahead of him. We had that conversation many times throughout the years but, as much as I tried to put her mind at rest, she was equally convinced his death was imminent.

CHAPTER 2

THE CALL

Another holiday season came and went, leaving echoes of memories abandoned in time. The innocence of setting cookies out and watching the children fall asleep while waiting for Santa is a cherished, but distant memory. Splitting time equally between divorced parents took its toll and the monsters were eager to return to their respective universities.

Aside from Nic's desperate need of a haircut and Tiffany's wanting a new cell phone, both were doing as well as expected for the typical cash-strapped student. Tiffany's love of history and her passion for children made her a natural for a career in teaching. Economics was Nic's preferred choice, and he was scheduled to study abroad in Ireland during the upcoming summer months.

We enjoyed a good visit, even though Nic departed a little early to return to his much celebrated Aggie Land. His love for Texas A&M seemed to outweigh family and holidays to a point that he wanted to be there 24/7. Most students felt homesick after spending so much time away from the comforts of their own bed, but it was totally opposite with Nic. He felt "school sick" when being away from A&M for any extended period of time.

Prior to his leaving, I lavished tireless teasing about his being an Aggie and he responded by saying, "Dad, what do they call an Aggie after graduation?"

I had no idea and he relished the opportunity to blurt out, "Boss! That's what they call us Aggies. Boss!"

Smiling and conceding to his overconfident Aggie pride, I added with sarcasm, "Yeah, right."

About a month later, I received a call that changed my life forever.

When my cell phone rang, I viewed the caller ID and at first hesitated to answer it.

"Greg!" came blaring in my ear and all I could think was, *What does she want this time?*

Divorced for nearly two years, I met any contact with my ex-wife with unresolved suspicion and skepticism. After twenty-three years of marriage, no divorce decree could erase the mistrust that still existed between us. We struggled to find any cordial words so we avoided any reason to contact each other.

Unless it had something to do with the monsters.

"Wuz up?" The tone of my response suggested I was annoyed at receiving the call.

Her voice was highly elevated, which was very unusual, considering the infrequency of our conversations. "You have a minute? It's about Nic."

My assumption was correct. *Oh God, what a relief!* How gratifying to know the conversation wasn't going to be about money or how I mistreated her. Nor did I have to listen to any more outlandish threats.

With nothing further to argue about, I could think of no reason my heart still raced with anxiety. If her call indeed concerned Nic, it could only be about a couple of ordinary problems he faced from time to time, his car needed some sort of repair, or he needed some extra cash. If that was the reason, why didn't he just call me himself? So, once again, I felt somewhat suspicious of the true nature of her call.

"Greg, I just received a call from Kevin, one of Nic's roommates. Nic has been taken to the local hospital. They're not sure what's wrong, but they suspect it could be serious."

"What! What could be so serious that he needed hospitalization?"

"At this point, I don't know a thing besides what Kevin told me."

Without any more skepticism, my voice now matched her level of pitch. "Was he in a car accident? Did something happen at his job? Wha... what the hell does 'serious' mean?"

"Again, Greg, I don't know. Kevin said he will call me back when he got more information, but I'm not going to wait. I'm leaving work now and driving to the hospital in College Station. You can join me if you want."

Although we were barely on speaking terms, it just didn't make any sense for us both to drive separately. At this point, all our issues should be irrelevant and we needed to get to College Station ASAP.

"Of course I'm going. Let's meet at a central location. I'm at Home Depot right now and I need to return to my job briefly. I'll meet you at the Walmart's parking lot by your office in about 45 minutes."

"Okay, see you soon."

"Bye."

Being a decent handyman, Home Depot is my drug of choice and where I spend hours researching my next project. Following the call, my crown molding project was suspended for the time being. In haste, I returned the chop saw to the shelf and exited the store within seconds. After racing back to the university, I informed my boss of my need to leave right away. He got no details other than it was a family emergency.

Appreciative for the lack of questions, I was in and out in less than ten minutes. With the university narrowing in my rear view mirror, I was flying trying to get to Walmart. Thank God the call was around noon and the traffic was light. Morning and afternoon traffic in Houston, Texas, is among the top five worst in the country.

My mind darted all over the place trying to determine what "serious" could possibly mean. If he wasn't in a car or workplace accident, what in the world could it be? With such uncertainty, only the most frightening possibilities came to mind. It's like receiving that dreaded phone call in the middle of the night and in an instant, you know something terrible has occurred.

Fighting those thoughts as best I could led me to say a quick prayer. "God, I have no idea what's taking place with Nic, but I ask that you keep him safe from all harm. Protect him from evil and any sickness. Please give the doctors the knowledge they need to treat him. These things I ask in Jesus name. Amen."

During my drive, I focused on believing that Nic's condition couldn't be anything more than a bad case of food poisoning, an adverse reaction to some medication, or maybe even alcoholic poisoning from binge drinking. In either situation, a visit to the hospital is warranted, but he would be okay after treatment.

The thought of drugs was also a possibility I couldn't ignore. Well aware he smoked pot on occasion, I would be shocked to discover anything more than that. It's not uncommon for college students to try an assortment of drugs, hoping to find the "right" high. I wasn't naïve to think Nic wouldn't play Russian roulette with drugs, but I felt desperate hope this wasn't the cause of his sudden hospitalization.

Without enough information to know his true condition, my staying positive was a must. Unfortunately, and like most people, my mind zeroed in on the negative.

My NASCAR-paced driving brought me to

Walmart's parking lot ahead of Arlene, so I called to check her status. "Hey, I just got here and I'm calling to see if you're close by."

"Yes, I'm almost there."

Fear heightened the tension in her voice. "I just received a follow up call from Kevin and he said the doctors believe Nic has meningitis."

Even having heard the term before, I was clueless as to what it meant. Maybe it was a severe case of the flu.

"What exactly is meningitis?"

"I don't know, Greg, but Kevin thought it was the milder version of the disease. He said there are two types, viral or bacterial. They believe he has viral meningitis, which is the milder version."

High-pitched and hurried, her panicked voice didn't appear to receive comfort from the milder version of the diagnosis. Right away I went into the "everything will be okay" mode and asked her to hang up the phone and concentrate on driving.

"But there's more I have to tell you!!"

"I know and you will soon, but you need to calm down right now. We don't need to complicate matters by your having an accident."

"I just exited the freeway and I see you. Bye."

She screeched into a parking place and exited her SUV with the determination of mother on a mission. She approached me with a look I had never seen in all the twenty-seven years of knowing her. Her eyes were wide open and their expanded whiteness represented a look of sheer desperation. We shared no hug, smile, or polite greeting exchange. Under the present circumstances, we found no room for pleasantries. She was petrified with fear and in no condition to drive.

"C'mon, Arlene, we'll take my car. Hopefully, we'll be back tonight or sometime tomorrow."

"It won't be tonight."

"We don't have all the details just yet, so let's not get too ahead of ourselves. Do you have everything you need?"

"Yes, I think so."

"Okay, let's go."

During the hour-and-a-half drive to College Station, we had lots of time for Arlene to relax before filling me in on the details. I asked her to take a couple of deep breaths, but it did little to relieve her agitated state of mind.

"So tell me everything Kevin said."

"He said Nic woke up with a very bad headache. It was so bad that he went to the campus clinic to be treated. They examined him and his symptoms suggested he had the flu."

Arlene took an extended exhale, giving herself a moment to recall all the details. "They gave him some Tylenol and sent him back home to rest. When he awoke several hours later, he was very incoherent and needed immediate attention." She bowed her head, avoiding my baffled stare. "Kevin called an ambulance, which took Nic to the nearest hospital. After he was admitted, the doctor said they suspected it was meningitis, but they were not sure what type."

With a hopeful smile, she raised her head and made direct eye contact. "They believe its viral meningitis, and if so, he should recover just fine after being treated."

No words came to me, but I understood why she was so hysterical. After taking in what she said, I needed to know the actual definition of meningitis. As my fear increased, I heeded the same advice I had given Arlene earlier and took a couple of deep breaths. As with her, my breathing at a slow rate had no effect my growing anxiety.

She Googled meningitis with my cell phone and what she read almost caused me to pull over.

Meningitis is a relatively rare infection that affects the delicate membranes that cover the brain and spinal cord. Bacterial meningitis can be contagious among people in close contact. Viral meningitis tends to be less severe, and most people recover completely. Bacterial meningitis is an extremely serious illness that requires immediate medical care. If not treated quickly, it can lead to death within hours -- or lead to permanent damage to the brain and other parts of the body. *WebMD*

Neither of us said a word. The definition stunned us beyond the point of communication. As much as I tried, I found no escape from the words, "death within hours." They kept repeating as an endless loop and my mind was helpless to stop it. No motion, no sound, no breathing, no consciousness, as if someone hit the pause button on the remote control of our lives and everything came to a screeching halt.

It seemed like hours, but in fact only minutes, passed before I whispered in a confident tone, "God is in control and he will see Nic through this."

Although a lukewarm Christian, my faith in God would be the only assurance to keep me from losing it. Other than faith, the one consolation we grasped at was the viral version diagnosis. If confirmed, Nic had a hopeful and realistic chance of full recovery. A bacterial diagnosis was an alternative I couldn't bear to consider.

The drive to A&M wasn't particularly scenic, but on occasion, it offered moments of distraction. The hilltop homes, with livestock roaming through vast prairies, were reminiscent of a time long ago when life seemed much simpler. The country stores and barbecue shacks awaited eager patrons in the form of busy city folk passing through.

With us both in deep thought about all the what-ifs, our conversational mood grew quiet. Earlier, to eliminate any diversions, I had turned off the radio when we left Houston. The only sounds were 18-wheelers going in the opposite direction. As they passed by, the desolate silence between us amplified the roar of their engine and vibration.

Then, out of nowhere, Arlene's cell phone rang. We twisted to face one another and our eyes revealed the fear that was hidden in our thoughts. We both knew the call could only be Kevin or the hospital.

Arlene grabbed her phone. "Hello" and after a few "Uh hums" she told the caller we should be there in thirty minutes. She thanked them for calling and repeated the somber news to me. "Greg, that was the emergency room and they just completed a spinal tap."

With her voice cracking, she delivered the message we had silently prayed against. "Their original diagnosis was wrong. Nic has bacterial meningitis and they're treating him with antibiotics to fight it. The doctors are also giving him steroids to push the drugs quickly through his system. They're doing all they can, but they want us to know how bad the situation really is. He ended the conversation by saying 'if you are praying parents, now is that time.'"

The reality of her statement was inconceivable and I had no response. Surely, we had no reason to believe our beloved son wouldn't recover from the meningitis attack, and the possibility of his dying was completely out of the question. No way would I allow that thought to enter my consciousness, but recognizing the fear in Arlene's eyes, I suspected she had already considered the doctor's words.

We were about to be in the fight of our lives, and to win it, we needed to be on the same page, which meant staying positive and rejecting any and all negative thoughts. I reached across the armrest between us and cradled her trembling hand in mine.

"As Christians, we've been taught all our lives that if we accept Jesus Christ as our Lord and Savior, then we are saved by God's grace and mercy. That applies to Nic as well. We have also been taught to have faith at all times, even when things appear hopeless. God is with us and he will see Nic through this. At this point, that's all we have and we have to pray and trust in God unconditionally."

"I have faith Greg, but—"

Motioning my hand in a stop position, I spoke in stern, but polite terms. "Absolutely no buts. Trust God and don't allow any other thoughts to enter your mind that are contrary to Nic being completely healed."

CHAPTER 3

DAY ONE

I completed the last leg of my NASCAR race without incident, yet my mind experienced a crash of emotions. While pulling into the hospital's parking lot, my fear of uncertainty waged war with my hopeful expectations. Nic's unexpected battle with life and death created a level of stress that was totally foreign to me. A pinched nerve in my shoulder from a high school football injury required an immediate massage. Grimacing in pain, I struggled to shift my car's transmission into park.

"What's wrong?" Arlene said while preparing to exit.

"After living together for twenty-three years, you don't know?"

"Your shoulder again?"

"Bingo. When I'm stressed it acts up, and right now it feels like someone's stabbing me repeatedly. But I'm fine. Let's go."

The "knife" in my shoulder joined forces with the chaos in my mind as we hurried through the

Emergency Entrance doors and proceeded to the admittance desk. Hospitals have a distinctive smell to them as if they all use the same disinfectant cleaner and this one was no different. The floors were freshly buffed and looked wet from the wax used to create a mirror-like shine. The walls of the corridors were an unusual bright white and were void of any stains or accidental smudges. Either the custodial crew had just finished cleaning or the hospital was sending a message that cleanliness is paramount to quality health care. Several people lingered in the waiting room, but none appeared to be students or roommates of Nic.

We approached the attendant behind the desk and introduced ourselves as parents of Nicolis Williams, a recently admitted patient. He had been moved from the emergency room to ICU. After a brief walk, we arrived and addressed the first nurse we encountered. "We're the parents of Nicolis Williams."

Without any further introduction or delay, a nurse immediately took us to a small private waiting room.

Hospitals only extended this courtesy when the situation was very serious, but somehow, it still didn't register how bad Nic's situation was. I was fearful the smaller room was where they put families whose loved one was near death.

The room was a far cry from the sterile corridors. Decorated with earth-toned colors, it was much more inviting and had a family room feel to it. The brown leather seating could accommodate about eight people comfortably and it correlated to a tee with a light shade of green captured in the pictures and walls. Centered in the room was a traditional style wooden table with lots of reading materials to keep its occupants distracted.

The room had two doors, one that opened to the larger waiting room and one that opened to ICU ward where Nic was being treated. The larger waiting room accommodated forty people or more and suggested to the waiting loved ones that the conditions of the patients were much less critical. A large television helped pass the time, while our waiting room suggested time was a precious commodity and it shouldn't be wasted on thoughtless entertainment. For obvious reasons, I preferred to be in the larger waiting room.

We paced the floor for about twenty minutes until the doctor arrived. He was a tall, slender man in his late forties with curly blond hair that accented his yellow polka-dot bow tie. The excessive lines embedded in his forehead and the matter-of-fact look on his face expressed the seriousness of Nic's condition.

"Mr. and Mrs. Williams, my name is Dr. Cunningham and I'm the physician treating your son."

With both of his palms raised and implying a slowdown motion he continued, "I know you have lots of questions, but please allow me to fill you in on what we know so far."

In no uncertain terms, I understood his request

for us to wait before asking anything, but after almost three hours of being in the dark, I couldn't help but interrupt. Standing toe-to-toe and scrutinizing his expression, my questions came out in a rapid-fire action. "How is he? Is he responding? Is he showing any signs of improvement? Is he conscious? When can we see him?"

"Mr. Williams, please, allow me to finish before I answer your questions."

"I'm sorry, it's just that we don't know anything and we have tons of questions. Go ahead, I won't interrupt again."

"When Nicolis arrived at the hospital, he was conscious, but very incoherent and a little combatant. He lost consciousness and went into a coma after about eight minutes following his arrival. His roommate filled us in about his trip to the campus clinic earlier this morning where he complained of a constant headache, fever, and dizziness."

Dr. Cunningham took a seat as he motioned us to join him. "These symptoms are commonly associated with the flu, but they are also the same symptoms associated with meningitis. We wanted to know if he had other symptoms like a stiff neck, body rash, or if he was sensitive to light."

I listened for every detail as Dr. Cunningham placed emphasis on the symptoms.

"His roommates didn't know and because Nicolis was unconscious, we performed a spinal tap to confirm our suspicions. Spinal fluid should be clear, but his was very cloudy." Dr. Cunningham's voice slowed as he pushed back his wire-framed glasses. "The test confirmed he has bacterial meningitis and we needed to act very quickly in treating him because the disease spreads very quickly. We are administering antibiotics along with large doses of steroids to accelerate the drug throughout his body. Every second counts with this disease, so we hope the steroids will speed up the treatment."

Dr. Cunningham avoided eye contact as he continued. "Lastly, I want to be completely honest with you. Your son's condition is very, very serious and it is a high probability he will not survive."

I was in total disbelief and shock at what the doctor had just disclosed. He might as well had been speaking a foreign language because the reality of his statement was incomprehensible. You just don't go from being a perfectly healthy twenty-year-old to "may not survive" in a few short hours.

The phone call we had received earlier was disturbing, but I believed the hospital was using that 'ole customer service' tactic of giving us the terrible news up front. And, by the time we arrived, the dramatic story would change to how Nic was miraculously responding due to their heroic efforts.

Wishful thinking on my part... No tactic was employed, no games played, and the seriousness of Nic's condition represented the authenticity of a parent's worst nightmare, the possibility of their child's death.

As a society, we've grown so accustomed to seeing

horrendous stories daily on television that we've become almost immune to them. Crazed gunmen murdering schoolchildren, babies dying after being left in car seats for hours in the smothering heat, or police killing unarmed citizens are just a few that get our attention. We watch in horror and we sympathize with victims and their families because of our humanity, but we can't imagine ourselves being in such a terrible situation. In our private thoughts we're thankful it's someone else and not us.

Arlene and I didn't have that luxury.

"Doctor, wait just a second, what do you mean, he may not survive?"

"Bacterial meningitis spreads very rapidly throughout the body and brain. When treated early, the chances of survival is much greater, but there could still be brain damage or loss of limbs or even both. We don't know at this point how advanced the disease has spread, but we're doing everything we can to stop it."

Out of frustration and fear, I shouted, "This is just crazy! He was fine just a couple of days ago and now he could die?"

"Mr. Williams, unfortunately with this disease, yes, he can."

Jumping up, I continued my inquiry. "Do you know how he got it? Has there been anyone else reported?"

Sensing my anger, Dr. Cunningham stood and placed his hand on the same shoulder I was experiencing throbs of pain. Arlene stood as well. "Mr. Williams, we don't know how he got it. It could spread by kissing or drinking after someone. In some cases, the victim carries the bacteria in their nose or throat and it becomes active for no apparent reason. To my knowledge, no additional cases have been reported."

The "hand on the shoulder" approach soothed my anger somewhat and Dr. Cunningham removed his hand as I continued. "You mentioned you're using steroids to push the antibiotics quickly throughout his system. How long before you know if it's working?"

"I've ordered some test that will reveal his brain activity and that should tell us a lot. It will be a few hours before we know anything definitive. Understandably, you have more questions, but I really need to get back to your son."

With a sense of desperation, I enclosed his right hand in both of mine and I pleaded with him. "He's our only son, please, please do all you can."

"I promise, Mr. Williams, we're doing everything we can to save him."

"Thank you."

"I'll see you later and hopefully we will have some better news."

Having never been in a situation like that before, my instincts told me we needed to pray for Nic. Not only Arlene and I, but all our family and friends needed to know the severity of the situation and they needed to pray as well.

As a Christian, my faith had never been tested

to that degree, but with my son's life at risk, we had no time to waste. With such negative news, his only chance of survival would require God's immediate intervention.

The faithful truly believe that when prayers go up, blessings come down. I was determined to do everything within my power to ensure that God would be bombarded with so many prayers that Nic's recovery would be considered a spiritual and medical miracle. My administrative skills kicked into gear and several tasks were assigned to Arlene.

We called family members, friends, church members, neighbors, and coworkers, giving them the heartbreaking news. With each phone call, we asked everyone to pray and share the news with others so they would also pray for Nic. Everyone wanted to know more details than the basic information we shared, but our priority was to make as many calls as we possibly could. Our phones never stopped ringing and texts flowed nonstop. Before long, both the batteries were dead and neither of us had brought a charger.

With no method of communication, I recalled seeing a CVS pharmacy across the street and I headed there to buy a battery. As I exited through the automatic doors, in walked a young man I recognized, but had never met.

"Hello, Mr. and Mrs. Williams?"

"Yes."

"Hi, I'm Kevin, the guy who called you earlier. I'm

one of Nico's roommates."

We had seen pictures of Nic's roommates, but never had the opportunity to meet any of them. According to my son, all three were super smart and really good guys to room with. The only thing about them that bothered Nic a little was they liked the controversial talk show host, Glen Beck. I recall discussing the Glen Beck thing with Nic and although he disagreed with a lot of what Mr. Beck stood for, he respected his roommate's right to believe what they believed. I was so proud him. My generation would find great difficulty in sharing a house with three guys who followed a man many consider a borderline racist. His generation, the millennials, are so much more accepting of different perspectives, and thank God they are.

Arlene greeted Kevin with a hug. "Thank you so much for calling me and being there to call the ambulance."

"I'm really glad I was home to make the call. Do you have an update on how he's doing?"

"Bacterial meningitis is the diagnosis and there hasn't been any change since he was admitted."

"Do you mind if I pass along that information? Several of Nico's friends want to know."

"Sure, please do."

We told him everything we knew and we wanted him to share the news with friends and also ask them to pray for Nic. As we talked, I noticed Kevin had the same cell phone as mine. I inquired if he had a charger with him. He didn't, but he went home and brought it back about fifteen minutes later.

As insignificant as his gesture was, I felt confident it was no coincidence our phones used the same battery charger. Making phone calls was critical with requesting prayers on Nic's behalf. Kevin's sudden appearance was right on time! God knew what we needed and he provided. This was just the beginning of God's response to Nic's recovery.

Before our phones died, we talked with Tiffany at length, but we decided not to tell her the seriousness of Nic's condition. We asked her to leave school in San Antonio and get to College Station as soon as she could the next day.

With the charger, we were back in business, making phone calls and requesting prayers. The news about Nic had circulated throughout the university and several of his friends came by to visit. Out of caution for possibly spreading the disease, the doctors did not allow any visitors for the time being, which included Arlene and me. I complied for the moment, but wild lions stationed at his door would not prevent me from seeing him later that evening.

While we waited, the hospital staff checked on us often. We wanted coffee and lots of it. The caffeine provided a good stimulant and would soon work miracles for our endurance. Once they allowed us in that hospital room, we were not leaving his side.

As we waited on pins and needles for the doctor's return, the hospital's chaplain visited us. I wasn't sure if he was sent because of pending bad news or he just selected parties at random in the waiting room areas.

Regardless of his intent, we accepted his invitation with enthusiasm. We followed him out of the ICU and into another wing of the hospital. I found it a little surprising when we passed the chapel, thinking his office would be adjacent to it, but they were mutually exclusive.

He opened the door to his office and the setting was similar to any typical business office, furnished with a contemporary walnut-colored desk with pictures of his family, two padded guest chairs, a complementary bookcase, and a dusty artificial plant in a corner.

Having never visited a chaplain's office before, I assumed the décor would have a more religious ornamentation that included a crucifix hanging on a wall, a listing of the Ten Commandments, a picture of Jesus, and maybe even a place to kneel and pray. My assumptions were based on my Christian prejudices and I failed to consider other faiths the chaplain would encounter. His office was faith neutral, as it should be.

"Mr. and Mrs. Williams, my role as chaplain is to offer solace and encouragement as you face the medical challenges of your son. Please know that God has not abandoned you or Nicolis during this most difficult time. His love endures forever and he will see you through this ordeal. Now, if you don't mind, let's all join hands while I lead us in prayer."

Ahead of him with our expectations, we complied with his request.

"Dear Lord of Mercy and Father of Comfort, You are the One we turn to for help in moments of distress and times of need. I ask you to be with your servant Nicolis in this illness. Jeremiah 17:14 says Heal me Lord, and I will be healed. So then, we ask on Nicolis' behalf to heal him. In the name of Jesus, drive out all infection and disease from his body.

"Dear Lord, I ask you to turn this illness into strength, suffering into compassion, and pain into comfort. May Nicolis' parents trust in your love and hope in your faithfulness, even in the middle of this suffering. Let them be filled with patience and delight in your presence as they wait for your healing touch.

"Please restore Nicolis to full health, dear God. Remove all illness from his body by the power of your Holy Spirit, and may you, Lord, be exalted for the remainder of his life. As you heal and renew Nicolis, Lord, may he bless and praise you. All of this I pray in the name of Jesus Christ. Amen."

We talked with the chaplain a bit after he concluded his prayer and he assured us of his availability any time we needed his services. We thanked him, returned to the waiting room, and made more calls. As the afternoon progressed into evening, I believed with every cell of my body that God would answer our prayers and Nic would recover one hundred percent. Regardless of what the doctors claimed, I had to hold on to that belief and trust God unconditionally. If not, they might as well have given me a straightjacket and taken me to a padded cell.

About 7:00 p.m., Dr. Cunningham returned to provide us more information about Nic's condition, and again, his demeanor suggested the news wasn't encouraging. He didn't say much, but insisted we follow him to the office of Dr. Newsome, the area's neurologist.

Dr. Newsome served several hospitals in the area and luckily for Nic, he was on duty to assist with his treatment. Dr. Cunningham opened the door and introduced Dr. Newsome, a balding, middle-aged doctor whose hopeless look mirrored that of his colleague. If solemnity could be an odor, his office reeked with the scent.

After we exchanged introductions, Dr. Newsome explained in great detail how bacterial meningitis can attack the brain and the results of such an attack. We were appreciative for the education, but we had heard the same news earlier.

I was thinking, *blah, blah, blah,* when Arlene said in an impatient manner, "How does what you're telling us apply to Nic's situation?"

Both doctors appeared confused, as if to suggest, What more do we have to say before you get it?

"Mrs. Williams, we have taken several scans of your son's brain and we regret to inform you there is no activity."

They proceeded to show us scans of what a normal brain looks like and then they compared that scan to Nic's. Instead of appearing to be somewhat wavy, his scan revealed a solid mass, which indicated severe swelling.

My heart pounded with fear and once again, I couldn't believe what I was hearing. Desperate, I said, "Why not remove a section of his skull to allow his brain room to temporarily expand."

"Mr. Williams, if we did that, his brain would continue to expand with no possibility of returning to its normal size."

He then showed us what looked like normal blood vessels in the brain scan, but instead he pointed to three aneurysms that had ruptured. This alone would cause instant death, but he went even further to convince us there was no brain activity.

"Your son's brain was so swollen that it forced his brainstem into his spinal column. I'm extremely sorry, but Nicolis cannot recover from this condition. He has no brain activity."

Tears formed in my eyes and my heart stopped beating, but somehow I still functioned. The room fell silent as the doctors waited for a response, but how do you respond to news that defies common sense and all rational thought? How do you even process that the sun will no longer shine or that the earth has depleted its oxygen supply?

Disbelief was an understatement. *How could my*

son have gone from having a headache to dying in a matter of hours? My mind told me it wasn't possible and I would not accept what they said to us.

I appreciated their candor and everything they were doing, but I told them in a calm voice, "My son is not brain dead. Do what you have to do, but he is not brain dead."

With no reason to continue the conversation, we demanded to see Nic.

"Mr. and Mrs. Williams, we're doing all we can, but—"

"No!" I yelled. "He's not brain dead, he just can't be. Please take us to him. Now!"

The doctors conceded to our demands for the time being and took us to Nic's room. Because his condition carried the likelihood of contagion, we were required to wear rubber gloves and a surgical mask. At this point, my safety became irrelevant, but I put on the protective garments and entered the room, scared to my core of what we were about to face.

My heart broke as I walked in and saw the respirator forcing breaths in and out of his body. All the tubes entering his body and the various monitors confirmed he was already on life support systems. What I saw shredded my heart even further, yet I had to hold it together. Not sure if he could hear me, I wanted to express confidence that all would be fine.

"We're here now, big guy, and everything will be okay, but you gotta fight, Nic. You gotta give it everything you got. The doctors are doing all they can, so don't give up! We're going to do everything humanly possible and with God's intervention, we'll get through this together. We love you so much. All our families, friends, coworkers, and the whole Aggie student body are praying for you, so you gotta do your part."

We sat for hours just talking to him, hoping he could hear us. At first, I struggled with keeping my emotions in check, but somehow, after visiting with him, an inner strength emerged, and the determination I needed to save my son would not be denied. Regardless of everything the doctors told us, I was more than convinced of Nic's recovery.

In fact, I was confident. Armed with nothing more than my faith, I was prepared to fight the battle till my last breath. Nic was going to come home healthy and whole.

As the night approached, Arlene's best friend, Leonora Hunte, and Nic's godmother, Deborah LeBlanc, arrived at the hospital to offer their encouragement. Arlene and Leonora had met in college and worked together for years at a title company. She's from Trinidad and even though she's been in the States for decades, she maintained her very enchanting and sultry Caribbean accent.

Like most Americans, I'm intrigued by foreign accents and I could listen to her talk all day. Throughout our divorce, Leonora was rock solid in support of Arlene, which deepened the impenetrable bond between them.

Deborah LeBlanc was our next-door neighbor, whom we met about two years before Nic was born. With a Cajun surname like LeBlanc and being from Louisiana, I assumed crawfish boils would be my weekly entertainment. As the only African American families on the block, we developed a close and lasting friendship. Our relationship expanded so much in those two short years that we named Deborah and Floyd, her husband, as Nic's godparents.

Arlene didn't want to leave Nic, but I convinced her it was okay to take a break. If she got some rest then, she could relieve me later. It was important for him to know at least one of us would always be with him. She agreed to leave, but planned on returning later that night.

Earlier in the day, Arlene had received several healing scriptures from the grief ministry at her church. She was instructed to repeat the scriptures while standing over Nic and be assured that God would respond. I was so encouraged by her church's involvement, and their actions solidified my belief that God would answer our prayers. Since the moment they received the news, they had called with prayers and nonstop support.

Arlene belonged to Windsor Village United Methodist Church, the largest Methodist church in America. After the divorce, I decided to leave the church because I felt too uncomfortable seeing Arlene every time I attended services. Being a new member of Lakewood Church, I was not familiar with the ministries or services available, so I didn't contact them for support.

Nic looked as if he were sound asleep and could wake up at any minute, craving his favorite powered doughnuts. He needed a trim and a shave, but aside from that, he appeared perfectly normal. It felt surreal to believe just a few hours earlier he was no different than the other 48,000 students on campus, going about their daily routines. I could almost hear his baritone voice saying, "Wuz up, Dad!"

I cried and cried while holding his hand, hoping our prayers would be answered. Of course, his expression was motionless, but I imagined seeing his beautiful smile once again. No way God would allow this to be Nic's fate, and if this were a test of my faith, I was all in. Nothing would prevent me from trusting God to heal my son. Nothing! It would be a miraculous testimony of God's will and Nic's destiny.

As promised, Arlene returned and shared with me the scriptures she received from her church. We were in agreement that our faith was being tested and we needed to do all we could to maintain it. The chaplain allowed us to use his bible and as instructed, we stood over Nic and read aloud the following scriptures associated with healing:

Exodus 23:25; Psalm 103:3; Psalm 107:20; Psalm 118:17; Proverbs 4:20-23; Isaiah 41:10, 13; Jeremiah 30:17; Matthew 8:2-3; Matthew 8:17; Mark 11:23-24; Romans 8:11; Proverbs 3:7-8; Psalm 147:3

Isaiah 53:5; Jeremiah 17:14; Psalm 91:14; Acts 4:29-30; Matthew 9:21-22; James 5:16; 1 Peter 2:24

Of all the scriptures we read continuously, none more than Mark 11:23-24 penetrated my spiritual consciousness.

I tell you the truth, you can say to this mountain, May you be lifted up and thrown into the sea, and it will happen. But you must really believe it will happen and have no doubt in your heart. I tell you, you can pray for anything, and if you believe that you've received it, it will be yours. (NLT)

We read the scriptures over and over with a firm belief that our efforts hit the bulls-eye of God's promise. I felt somewhat strange to be working together with Arlene without a hint of drama whatsoever. I'm sure Nic was pleased we could set aside our differences in support of him. Around 10:00 p.m., we decided to take a break and I encouraged her to go visit with Leonora and Deborah while the hospital's night shift was coming on duty. The head nurse had allowed them to wait in a vacant ICU room adjacent to Nic's. This accommodation gave Arlene the opportunity to visit and still come in and relieve me from time to time.

Since we first arrived at the hospital, I was impressed with their consideration for our situation and their willingness to comfort us during the worst day of our lives. Even the horrific news from Dr. Cunningham was delivered with care and empathy. All of that first-rate customer service and bedside manner came to a sudden stop with the appearance of Dr. Okafor.

Sitting next to Nic and reading the scriptures, an African woman with a thick accent entered the room and introduced herself as Dr. Okafor, the nighttime physician assigned to the ICU.

"Mr. Williams, my name is Dr. Okafor and I will be treating your son tonight. How are you, sir?"

I paused in my reading and stood up to shake her hand. "It's nice to meet you, Dr. Okafor, but I wish it was under different circumstances. I've had much better days, but I'm coping as best I can."

"Yes, I read his charts and I'm so sorry we could not do more to prevent the advancement of the disease."

"The doctors showed us the brain scans and basically told us our son is brain dead. We totally reject the diagnosis regardless of what the scans show."

"Mr. Williams, it is very clear that your son's condition is—"

"Dr. Okafor, I'm telling you what I told the doctors earlier. We're Christians and we firmly believe in the healing power of God. We have put our complete trust in him and not the brain scans."

She went to his bedside and opened his eyelid. "Mr. Williams, please see that your son's pupil is fully dilated, which means there is no brain activity."

She then poked him in a couple of areas that should have produced a reflex movement, but his body did not respond. "Even in a comatose state, a patient's body will still react when touched in these areas."

"Dr. Okafor, I really don't give a damn about your opinion or anyone else's! You know what, you can leave now and don't bother coming back! You have no business treating my son."

"Mr. Williams, I'm sorry. It's really not my intent to upset you; however, as a physician, I have an obligation to be perfectly honest with you. I sincerely apologize if my comments offended you."

"Apology accepted, but I still don't want you treating my son. Just leave, please."

As she departed the room, she turned to me with a somber tone, "I want you to know that I too believe in God."

Maybe I was wrong for dismissing her, but her bedside manner was atrocious. Although she was only doing her job, she was oblivious to my state of mind, which was fragile at best. Arlene returned soon afterward and I told her what happened. She was just as angry and supported my decision to dismiss Dr. Okafor.

Arlene brought me up to date regarding the calls from everyone, but one in particular she wanted to talk with me about. Leonora's niece, Aisha, lives in New York City and she did some research on bacterial meningitis. She suggested we consider moving Nic to the medical center in downtown Houston. There, he may stand a better chance of recovery rather than at a regional hospital.

Considering the hopelessness from the hospital staff, a transfer sounded like a great idea. We hadn't received any encouraging news since the moment we stepped foot in the hospital. If the world-renowned Texas Medical Center would take Nic, we were prepared to move him.

My watch showed past 2:00 am and we both were exhausted, so we decided to continue the conversation in the morning. We went next door to say good night and to thank our friends for coming. They were already asleep, so Arlene took the remaining chair and pushed a switch that converted it into a bed. Within seconds, she sank into a deep sleep and I returned to continue praying.

Although I felt bone-tired like Arlene, the cups of coffee I downed earlier were having the desired effect. At some point during those early morning hours, I was supposed to trade places with her, but I decided against waking her. All night I stayed by Nic's bedside and prayed and prayed.

Prior to that night, no circumstance during my life ever required such concentration and determination. That day was the most exhausting time of my life, in emotion, mind, spirit, and body, yet I was confident of God's presence and his willingness to answer my prayers. As much as I trusted God, the fear of his not saving Nic lurked in the shadows of my mind.

What if he didn't? was a thought I forced out of my head, but it always returned. Did that mean my faith was not 100% and if not, would that cause God to abandon Nic? The bible speaks of being able to move mountains, if one has the faith of a mustard seed. For certain, my faith was much larger than a mustard seed, but to ensure Nic's recovery, I was willing to do anything and everything God could demand of me.

As the night descended, my need for sleep made my eyelids feel like ten-pound weights. I gave in, hoping the nightmare would end with me awakening at home and thanking God that all that transpired was just a horrible dream. A very vivid dream, but still a dream.

I pulled a chair next to Nic's bed, laid my head near his arm, told him I loved him, and let nature take its course.

CHAPTER 4

DAY TWO (a.m.)

Through the glass wall that separated our adjoining rooms, I watched Arlene awaken with a prolonged yawn. Her outstretched arms and a grimace on her face made it very apparent she hadn't slept well. Hospital beds aren't the most comfortable, but even a presidential suite of a five-star hotel wouldn't have helped her. Absorbing the graveness of Nic's condition far outweighed the comfort of sleep.

She covered her mouth as she struggled to silence her yawn, hoping not to disturb her faithful companions. As her arms fell to her side, she displayed a strange look. I suspected the conversation about the transfer interrupted her slow awakening and demanded immediate attention.

She had an acute awareness that if there was any chance of saving our son, he required the very best medical care available. Although the staff was trustworthy and competent, except for Dr. Okafor, doubts lingered that Nic wasn't receiving every option available to him. The hospital was a first class facility, but paled in comparison to the hospitals located in Houston's famed Texas Medical Center. Sitting by and believing prayer alone was going to save Nic wasn't sufficient. Prayer indeed changes outcomes, but as James 2:17 says, *Faith without works is dead.*

Work in this instance meant doing whatever it took to get the transfer completed.

Arlene entered the room sometime around 6:00 a.m. "Good morning, Greg"

"Good morning."

"Was there any change last night?"

My eyes felt on fire from the lack of sleep myself, but I was awake. A strong cup of java would no doubt get me going.

"No. Nothing to report. Another doctor came in a couple of hours ago to check Nic's status. Before he approached him, I asked did he believe in God and he said he couldn't be a doctor if he didn't. Apparently, he'd seen too many miracles over the years for him not to be a believer. I hope this is one more he can add to the list. He did confirm, however, no change in Nic's condition."

She sat on edge of the bed and leaned over to kiss Nic on the cheek, "Good morning, little man."

Then she turned to face me. "So you wanna transfer him to the Medical Center?" She asked with a bit of uncertainty in her voice.

I shouted, "Hell, yeah!" as I threw my hands up in jubilation. "If they can't help him there, then no one can. This is a matter of life and death and we have to consider every possibility. You sound like you're not sure, Arlene."

Pointing to her chest, she said, "Oh, I'm one hundred percent sure, but I just didn't know how you felt about it."

"Well, that should be expected since we haven't been on the same page the last couple of years." Shaking my head in disappointment, I continued, "I couldn't live with myself if Nic died and we didn't try even a remote possibility to save him. For all we know, this is part of God's plan, so we gotta give it a try. As much as I prayed last night, there wasn't any assurance that Nic would recover, but that doesn't mean my faith isn't strong."

I paused a couple seconds to emphasize my position. "Let me be clear. It is, but I also believe we have to do all in our power and trust God will do the rest."

"Okay, I'll call Aisha and tell her to make inquiries about a transfer."

"You mentioned that Aisha is Leonora's niece, but who is she really?"

"Not sure, but I know she lives in New York and she's very knowledgeable about meningitis. She offered to help anyway she can, so let's see what she can do. Who knows, she just may be the angel sent to help us."

"No argument from me. At this point, we need a miracle."

The day would be extremely busy with the transfer, keeping everyone in the loop, and breaking the news to Tiffany. She was to arrive around noon so we had the added challenge of making a trip to Houston and back before she got in town. Taking a shower and packing a change of clothes was an unavoidable necessity.

Like many siblings, the 'monsters' were highly competitive and taunted each other every chance they got, but even so, they shared a deep and genuine love for one another. Several weeks back during our Christmas meal together, they had teased each other about the universities they attended. Tiffany accused Texas A&M of brainwashing their students and complained of how ridiculous Aggies sound when they acknowledge each other with their crazy "Whoop" chant.

On the other hand, Nic harassed Tiffany about UTSA not having a football team and it being the stepsister of the University of Texas in Austin. Their merciless attacks to belittle each other and the other's institution gave their extended families a huge laugh. However, beyond the entertaining smoke screen, they had each other's backs. They were never openly affectionate with one another, but the love and respect had been just as apparent as the insults and criticisms.

I visited the nurse's station to give instructions, should Tiffany arrive before we returned, and Arlene went back to tell Leonora and Deborah of our plan. I was happy beyond measure they were there to support us. God knows we needed it. I remained in the corridor, returning calls to my family, where I overheard Arlene's conversation.

Hesitant to wake her best compadres, she whispered, "Good morning, ladies."

Leonora woke up right away and yawned while Deborah needed a little nudge prior to sitting up in the combination bed/chair.

"Greg and I are headed back to Houston to clean up and pack for a few days stay. We plan to return before Tiffany arrives which should be around noon."

Deborah eyes grew wide with much expectancy. "Is there any change with Terrell?"

She's the only person who calls Nic by his middle name.

"No, no change at all for now. That's why we've decided to transfer him to a hospital in the medical center. We hope he may have a better chance at recovery at a larger, better-equipped hospital. Leonora, we want you to contact Aisha and tell her to move forward with arranging the transfer. We're not comfortable telling the doctors here just yet, but they'll find out soon enough."

Leonora answered with her traditional Caribbean response, "No problem, mon. I will give her a call in a few. If there's any additional information she needs besides what you gave me last night, I'll call you."

"Thanks a bunch. I know y'all need to get back as well, so we'll return as soon as we possibly can."

With the bed now fully converted into its chair

position, Deborah said, "Don't worry about us. Go do what you guys gotta do and we'll work on the transfer."

"Greg left word at the nurse's station that we'll be out of pocket this morning for a few hours, but if there is any change in Nic's condition, they should call us immediately. Thank y'all for staying with me last night. You have no idea how much it means to me and I thank God for you both."

Mouthing the words "good-bye," Deborah led Arlene by the hand and pulled her to the door to leave. "Get out of here and go take care of your business. We'll see you when you get back and hopefully have some good news by then."

Arlene gave them both big bear hugs, held each of their hands, and thanked them again for being there.

I resumed my NASCAR driver role and we sped away, headed home to take care of a few but much needed errands. Our plan was to stop by my job first; go to my home next to pack; pick up Arlene's car from Walmart; and then follow her home so she could pack, and then we would return to College Station. The round trip required us to be in close proximity for about four hours and I hoped our unified concern for Nic would serve to overcome our mistrust of each other. We hadn't spent that much time together since before the divorce, but with Nic's condition posing as a constant mediator, our differences were nonexistent for the time being.

The first leg of our trip was quiet with expectation

except for the occasional hunger pain screaming for any form of nourishment. By focusing so much attention on Nic, we had forgotten to eat and our stomachs reminded us that our bodies needed energy.

"Hey, old lady, I hear your stomach growling up a storm over there. Wanna stop briefly and get something to eat?"

"Nah, I'm good. I'll eat something when I get home."

"You sure?"

"Yeah, I don't want to stop unless we absolutely have to. We have to return before Tiffany gets to the hospital."

"Alrighty then."

That was the only exchange between us after leaving the hospital 40 miles back.

Trying to avoid the "elephant in the room" conversation about Nic, I attempted to steer our talk in a different direction. "Isn't it strange how you don't experience hunger when your mind is so preoccupied with something?"

"I guess, Greg."

She didn't bite and redirected our exchange back to the only subject that mattered, Nic. She said in a half-hearted voice, "How did you sleep last night?"

"Not a wink and I'm feeling it now. I kept repeating the scriptures until I couldn't any longer. Not sure when, but I fell asleep at some point. How about you?"

"No, I didn't either. Just too many negative

thoughts going through my mind. I'm scared, Greg."

"So am I, but we have to stay strong in our faith."

"I must admit I'm really surprised at you and your newfound commitment. For someone who attends church only out of obligation, I'm amazed at your willingness to express your faith. I guess something must have finally penetrated that thick skull of yours."

We both laughed, a welcome change of pace compared to all the doom and gloom we received since we arrived in College Station.

"Oh, you have jokes, I see. Honestly though, now I understand why so many people become converted while incarcerated."

Determined to make a point, I lowered the volume of the music playing and tried to maintain eye contact. "When you're at rock bottom, nowhere else to turn, abandoned and without hope, you reach for the only hand extended to you, Jesus Christ. He's there welcoming you into his loving arms. I was always critical of people who discovered Jesus in that manner, but that was wrong."

Arlene pointed towards the speedometer as a reminder to watch how fast I was driving. By activating the cruise control, I calmed her concern and continued with my revelation. "Whatever the circumstances, it shouldn't matter why one accepts Christ in their life. Their acceptance is celebrated by the angels in heaven, so who am I to criticize them? Like the prisoners, there is no one else to turn. The medical reports don't give Nic any chance of recovery, so my faith in God is all I have and I am expecting a miracle."

She looked perplexed at me for a few seconds and then turned to stare at whatever passed her window. If her thoughts were verbalized, they would say, *Who the hell is this person next to me?*

Our private thoughts resumed with no more discussions until I reached the first leg of our trip. After signing a few papers and taking a few moments to talk with my staff, I returned to my car and continued our trip home.

Arlene looked at me with more than a puzzled expression, more like a suspecting mother of a mischievous two-year old. Arlene said, "Greg, you okay?"

"Yeah, I am. I got a little emotional when updating my staff on Nic's situation. I'm not sure why it suddenly got to me. I think that damn doctor from last night is still having an effect on me."

"How so?"

"Trying to convince me that Nic died was so rude. She probably sees these situations on a daily basis, but what she did was unconscionable. I'm a little emotional, but I'm okay."

I continued, "God didn't bring him this far only to abandon him now. The healing scriptures from last night are God's promises and he will honor them. I can't admit to praying or reading the bible everyday but, I am a believer in God the Father, the Son, and the Holy Spirit. Like the prisoners, when there's nowhere else to turn, I'm thankful for the relationship with God, albeit a lukewarm one."

"So, you don't think what the doctor said is true?"

"No, they wouldn't intentionally lie to us. I just choose not to accept it. God is bigger than any negative brain scan or any other evidence they present."

"Greg, but what if—"

"We'll deal with whatever happens when it happens. For now, we have to fight the naysayers and pray for our son. Easier said than done, but that's all we can hold on to right now."

"Greg, remember when Nic was born and I kept asking you, did he have all his toes and fingers? I was so worried something would go wrong because of things I did in my past."

"I don't know much, but God doesn't work like that. Whatever sins we committed in our past were long since forgiven and forgotten. His mercy is bigger than any sin we committed. God allowed this to happen, but he didn't cause it to happen. Remember the story of Job? Satan had to get permission from God to do the things he did. Our situation is no different and like Job, we have to stay committed to our faith. Unsure how any of this will turn out, I'm putting all my trust in God and you should, too."

"Oh, I am, Greg, but I can't easily dismiss what the doctors told us."

During the next three stops, we each showered, ate some leftovers, packed enough clothes for a few days and returned to the hospital by 1:30 p.m. As I parked the car, I noticed a television van in the south end of the parking lot. It was hard to ignore with the antenna extended 40 feet in the air from the van's roof.

We entered the hospital through the ICU entrance and paused before we reached a packed waiting room. I looked at Arlene with suspicion for a moment before we continued through the ICU double doors and entered the private waiting room where Leonora was engaged in a telephone conversation.

Deborah rose from her seat to greet us. "Hey, I'm glad you guys made it back safely. A lot has been going on with the transfer, but we decided not to disturb you until everything was settled. Leonora is on the phone now with her niece trying to finalize the details."

That was good news indeed, but Nic's status was first and foremost on my mind. By not receiving any calls from the hospital could only mean there was no change, but still, I had to ask.

Noticing the eagerness with my inquiry, Deborah responded right away to ease my expectations. "Unfortunately, there hasn't been any change at all, but he has tons of friends who want to visit with him."

Pointing to the large crowd in the waiting room, I said, "Are all those people his friends?"

"Yes and many more of them were here earlier. They kept coming and coming until the hospital asked them to please leave enough seating for visitors of the other patients. It's like they're taking shifts and waiting until the next group arrives. And on top of that, a television crew is out there wanting to interview you."

"Interview us? Why?"

"Nic's situation is developing into a huge news story and it's getting lots of attention."

"Oh? Really, I guess that's a good thing, but my only concern right now is him getting better. I'm not sure how Arlene feels but I'm not doing any interviews."

"I'm with you," Arlene spoke up. "Getting Nic transferred is a top priority and anything else can wait for now. When Tiffany gets here, she can give the interview if she wants to.

Leonora finished her phone conversation and seemed very antsy to talk with us. Standing up and smiling from ear to ear, she made her announcement. "Hey, Love, I have some fantastic news! Aisha has been speaking with a lady named Anna Dragsbaek of The Immunization Partnership and she has some connections at Methodist Hospital in the Medical Center. It appears they will accept Nic, provided this hospital agrees with the transfer, but there has been some resistance on their part."

Excited by the news, I clenched my fist and pulled it back while shouting "Yes!" but I was confused as well. "Resistance! Why? If Methodist Hospital will accept him, no way in hell this hospital can keep him here. This is the first good news we've had since we set foot in this place. Not sure who I need to speak with to authorize the transfer, but it will happen and it will happen soon."

We thanked Leonora for her efforts and left for the nurse's station to speak with Dr. Cunningham or to whomever had the authority to approve the transfer.

Dr. Cunningham was still the doctor of record, but he was not available to speak with us at that moment. While waiting, we decided to go visit with Nic's friends in the waiting room. Because Tiffany had yet to arrive, we gave the nurse's station permission to allow visitation by his friends. It was a short walk from the station to the waiting room and as I slowly opened door, I was in awe and unprepared for the number of students gathered.

Gabby, a close friend of Nic's, had told us the night before how popular he was on campus, but I still found it incredible to believe that many students considered him their friend. For the second time that day, I was close to tears. My heart gushed with joy for him due to the many friendships he had developed during his brief time at A&M. For many years, he endured so much difficulty trying to make friends, but the memory of all that pain seemed light years away.

As the door closed behind us, I paused and scanned the room just to absorb all the friendly but saddened faces. Speechless by the sheer number of them, any negative thoughts I ever harbored against the university were in that moment erased from my consciousness forever. Seeing so many sincere students who cared about my son—for no other reason than for the person God created him to be—was a revelation of monumental proportions. The pigmentation of his skin color did not matter, not his ethnicity, nor his faith or his socioeconomic status. They were there solely out of love and support for their fun-loving and, hope-to-God not, dying friend. The students represented a wide spectrum of nationalities and their presence demonstrated a welcoming beacon in the lighthouse of diversity acceptance.

I took the opportunity to introduce us. "Hi, everyone. I'm Nic's father, Greg, and this is his mother, Arlene. Please excuse us if we look surprised, but we had no idea you all are here to visit Nic. Oh, I'm sorry… Nico. We found out last night he goes by Nico here at A&M. He did mention it to us before, but we never knew he chose to use it exclusively. You all can visit him soon, but before you do, we want to update you on his condition.

I paused and rubbed my eyes to impede the accumulation of tears destined to flow any second. "By now, you all know he has bacterial meningitis. The doctors are treating him with antibiotics and steroids. They're not very optimistic, but we're praying God will heal our son completely and we ask your prayers as well."

As I spoke, some background chatter came through, "For sure" and "Count on it."

I smiled as best I could. "When you visit him, please talk with him like you normally do. Engaging with him and hearing your voices may be the one thing that initiates his recovery."

The 50 or 60 students in attendance pushed the capacity of the room way past its limits. Girls, guys, various nationalities, and many wearing their spirited "Gig'm Aggies" attire, all were standing, listening and hanging on to every word of our update.

Arlene addressed them next. "Nico would be so excited to see all of you here for him. As you probably already know, he loves attention."

Someone shouted, "That's Nico for sure!" followed by lots of chuckles.

Arlene smiled. "We want to be completely honest with you. He is in the fight of his life and we're doing everything we possibly can to get him the best care available. While on our way here yesterday, the doctor told us, if you believe in prayer, now is that time. Well, we're repeating that same message to you. Please pray for your friend. For now, we have to get back to the doctors, but I have a question if you don't mind."

No one objected, so Arlene proceeded.

"How many of you have been vaccinated for bacterial meningitis?"

About one-third of the students raised their hands.

Arlene gasped at the low number. With raised eyebrows, she expressed a desperate plea. "Please, I beg you all to get vaccinated as soon as you can. We didn't know anything about the meningitis risk for college students, and to think, all this could have easily been avoided with a simple shot. So again, please, go get vaccinated and protect yourselves."

A few of them nodded and a couple raised their hands with questions. We accommodated them, but only briefly.

"We would like to meet and talk with each of you, but we're in the middle of something right now and we desperately need to get back to the doctors. Please feel free to go visit with your friend. We'll keep you informed of his condition as quickly as we know something. Again, we want to thank each and every one of you for visiting and for your prayers. Your presence makes a huge difference for Nico and for us as well. We'll be right next door if anyone needs us."

As we turned to leave, someone called out, "We love Nico and God will heal him."

I couldn't agree more and that sentiment was echoed by the collective "yeses" we heard from the group.

Before leaving the room, I looked back at Nic's friends in complete awe. I was very much unaware of his popularity on campus and the impact his condition would have on so many people. Texas A&M had become his family and they welcomed him with the open arms of a long lost friend.

In private, I had never wanted him to attend A&M because of its harsh racial history. In my day, it was not an institution that welcomed African Americans unless you were a superior athlete. All other black students were viewed as the university's attempt to fulfill a racial quota. Fellow students scrutinized you as illegitimate and thus taking the spot of a more qualified and deserving student. Whether true or not, this reputation of Texas A&M circulated for years within the "hood" where I grew up.

I knew my son well. His need to belong—to be accepted—was more valuable than the education he sought. I suspected his time at A&M would be a painful experience that would intensify his need for social acceptance. If my old perceptions turned out to be true, I wasn't even confident he would graduate.

Not knowing what to expect from A&M, I really didn't care. My mind was preoccupied to the fullest with trying to get Nic transferred, but seeing those students erased all my doubt and any insecurities I held against the university. The students represented everything Nic could ever have imagined. Everyone he met accepted and liked him, and that fulfilled a void he carried thus far in his life.

We returned to our small waiting room and found it filled to capacity. Arlene's mother, her sister-in-law, plus my sister and brother-in-law, all had arrived while we were visiting with Nic's friends. We greeted everyone and gave them an update regarding the transfer possibility. Tiffany hadn't showed up yet, but she called to let us know she would be there soon.

We were discussing the transfer when the door from the ICU corridor burst open. Dr. Cunningham walked in the crowded room with a look of confusion. He greeted us and asked if we had a few minutes to talk. The moment of truth had arrived and I suspected he wanted to discuss the transfer.

"Yes, of course," I said.

"Would you prefer to talk in my office?"

"Nah, this is fine. Everyone here is family."

"Okay. We have been contacted by Methodist Hospital in Houston about transferring your son there. Mr. and Mrs. Williams, we're adamantly opposed to transferring Nicolis. His condition is too fragile to consider moving him and there are just too many liability issues as well."

Struggling to subdue my contempt, I said, "Doctor Cunningham, what you just said doesn't make much sense to me at all. Your diagnosis from the beginning is that Nic has no brain activity, which essentially means he's brain dead. If so, how could his condition be considered fragile?"

"Moving him could cause further damage and determining who is responsible creates a liability issue for this hospital."

The doctor's years of experiencing dealing with irate family members had prepared him to remain calm. Good thing for him.

My frustrations, on the other hand, pushed the boundaries of civility. I took a step towards him to close the distance between us. He didn't budge, but clearly, he sensed my irritation.

With my voice nearing a shouting volume, I glared

at him. "Damn it, if he's already brain dead, what further damage could possibly be done by moving him?"

"Mr. Williams, I understand you want the very best treatment for your son and I assure you we've done everything medically possible to treat him. Transferring him to another hospital will not change the results of his current condition."

"You're right about one thing. We are trying to get the very best care for our son. That's our only concern and transferring him is not an insult to you or this hospital. If Methodist is willing to take him, then obviously, they must have an alternate treatment that may save our son."

"Again, there is no alternate treatment for bacterial meningitis. Antibiotics are the only effective method to treat the disease. If the patient is treated early enough, it is highly successful in preventing loss of limbs and loss of life. If the treatment is late and the disease has spread throughout the body and the brain, the results are life threatening. That's what we have here now. "

"I cannot question your medical knowledge, but again we're simply trying everything we possibly can to save him. The bottom line is this, if the Methodist Hospital is willing to take him, then we want him transferred. Period. There's nothing more to discuss."

"We don't recommend it, but we'll continue talks with Methodist. They have requested us to share the test results we've taken. After sending them, we'll see where things stand."

"Do what you have to do, but again, if they will take him, we want him transferred."

Dr. Cunningham departed the room wearing the same confused look with which he entered, which could only be attributed to our inability to acknowledge his belief that there was no hope. The facts speak for themselves and why we couldn't see the obvious was a mystery to him. From his vantage point, Nic's fate was sealed. Our faith dictated we hold on to God's promises, and no way we were giving up, regardless of what evidence they presented.

A couple hours went by without any contact from Dr. Cunningham or from Methodist Hospital. Pacing only exasperated my concern and I couldn't wait any longer.

Arlene and I decided to call Methodist. We called Aisha first for the contact information and she also informed us about conversations she had with Memorial Herman and St. Luke's Hospitals, in case things did not work out with Methodist. We were so thankful for her assistance and to think, we never even met her. She was a godsend and we now counted on her ability to work the system on our behalf. Confident God was putting the right people in place to assist, there was no way we would be denied.

I called a Ms. Robinson at the Methodist Hospital. "Hello, my name is Greg Williams and I'm contacting you regarding the transfer of my son Nicolis Williams from the local hospital here in College Station."

"Hello, Mr. Williams, your son's case has been

discussed, however; no decision has been made just yet."

"Can you tell me approximately when one will be made?"

"I can't say for sure. A thorough review of the patient's condition has to take place along with the treatment that has been administered to this point. After the analysis, if the doctors believe more can be done, the transfer will be approved."

"Is there anything I can do or talk with someone? We desperately want our son moved as soon as possible."

"I understand your concern, Mr. Williams, but all I can say officially is the case is being reviewed."

"Okay, we'll wait until we hear from you, but please call as soon as you know something."

"We'll be in touch."

"Thank you."

The conversation with Methodist Hospital wasn't what I expected and it left me feeling precarious at best. Somehow I had convinced myself they would be enthusiastic about Nic's situation and their approval would be granted without hesitation. After the call, I was even more appreciative of Aisha's attempts with the other hospitals.

While we waited for the "lifeline" call, Tiffany contacted us. She was about an hour outside of College Station and her call provided an opportunity to change our focus for a while.

We were very concerned about how to break the

news to her. She projects a very tough exterior, but inside she's very sensitive and can be emotional at times. I was happy to learn her boyfriend, David, was with her. He could be a huge shoulder to lean on after receiving the worst news of her life.

Once the call with Tiffany ended, a young man of about 35 years old entered the room and introduced himself as a representative of Southwest Transplant Alliance. Clean cut, dressed in khaki pants and a short-sleeved Polo shirt, he looked like a customer service representative sent to obtain a survey. He asked to speak with us in private and again, we declined.

At first, we didn't know the purpose of his visit and the term "Transplant" in his employer's name didn't register with either of us. But as he proceeded with his 'pitch,' I soon realized he was there to sell us on the idea of organ donation.

The speed of light was slow as a sleepy sloth in comparison to Arlene going from considerate to ballistic.

"How dare you come in here with the idea of donating organs!! This hospital may believe my son is dead but we don't!! He still has a chance and as long as we believe that, don't approach me about donating his organs."

"But, Ms. Williams, people are in desperate need of transplants and it would be such a waste—"

"I really don't give a damn about other people's needs. My son has his own needs and we're trying to do everything we can to address them. Just go! Get out now and don't come back. Even if we do get to that point, it won't be with you!!"

It was pointless to apologize, but he tried in earnest. I attempted to come to his defense, and Arlene snapped at me as well.

I didn't take it personally. She was on edge and so was I. Yesterday, she was a mother on a mission and, despite her best efforts, the mission was vanishing moment by moment.

As she opened the door to force his exit, a disturbing thought popped in my head. The hospital took a very calculated risk by allowing the organ donation people to approach us. Maybe they knew something we didn't.

It was time to call Methodist again.

Even as a past recipient of similar outbursts, I couldn't blame her now. I placed my hand on Arlene's shoulder. "You okay?"

"Yeah, I'm just pissed off at the guy for approaching us with that nonsense. They know we're trying to get Nic transferred and they allow this idiot to come in here and try to convince us to donate his organs. Really? How insensitive. No, how stupid!"

"It was very thoughtless on their part, but he was just doing his job."

"The hell with his job and you made matters worse by trying to defend him."

"I wasn't trying to defend him, but none of that's important right now. We need to call Methodist.

Think about it... No way would this hospital let that guy come in here unless they knew the transfer wasn't taking place."

"No, Greg, that just can't be right. Methodist said they would call."

"True, but we haven't heard from them and at least two hours have passed. How long does it take to determine if they can help or not? Somebody knows something and we're in the dark. I'm calling now."

"Maybe you're right, but I sure hope you're wrong."

Before making the call, Dave, my brother-in-law, wanted to say a prayer. Of the relatives in the room, he's a true man of God and I trusted God would hear and respond to his prayer. Thinking my "lukewarm" relationship with God wasn't sufficient, I couldn't afford to take any chances. At that critical juncture, the prayer baton was passed to Dave. We all formed a circle, held hands, and bowed our heads while he led us in prayer:

"Father God, we humbly approach you in Jesus's name. There is no other like you. Your authority and power is limitless. You said when two or three gather in your name, you will be among us. We feel your presence here right now and we acknowledge your love for us. Your Word says, 'With men this is impossible; but with God all things are possible.' We believe in your word and we ask that you intercede right now and bless this situation so Nic can be healed completely and restored to his loving family.

God, we specifically ask that you allow the transfer to take place and give the doctors the knowledge and ability to heal your child. Lord, we place this situation in your loving hands and we thank you for your grace and mercy. In Jesus' name we pray. Amen."

We thanked Dave for his prayer, but I wasn't sure if my heart was filled with assurance or fear regarding the pending call. Everything depended on that transfer and, as much as I wanted to believe God was about to answer our prayers, the thought of him not doing so terrified me.

My faith was solid, but my fears could not be denied. How did fear sneak in if my faith was supposed to be rock solid? By acknowledging my fear, would God refuse to act on Nic's behalf? Would the call end with me abandoning my faith and burying my son or with me celebrating God's awesomeness? The forces of dread and anticipation were intertwined, but only one of them could endure.

"Hello, Ms. Robinson, this is Greg Williams calling again to check the status of my son's transfer."

"Hello, Mr. Williams. Can I put you on hold for a second?"

"Sure, I can wait."

As I paced while holding the phone, the look on everyone's faces confirmed the significance of the call. Some expressions were joyous anticipation, while others revealed pending disappointment. Arlene's features expressed a desperation of hope and mine couldn't have been any different.

"Mr. Williams, has anyone called you from Methodist Hospital?"

"No, that's why I'm calling now."

"I'm so sorry, but I need to put you on hold again."

"I'll wait."

The waiting felt like torture with no end in sight, and I had no idea how long my sanity would hold up.

After a minute or so, a man's voice replaced Ms. Robinson's. "Mr. Williams, this is Dr. Langford with Methodist Hospital's transfer team. I apologize for us not contacting you. Obviously there was some miscommunication on our part."

"Apology accepted. So where are we with the transfer?"

"I'm so sorry to inform you, but unfortunately the transfer has been denied. After a thorough review of the brain scans, x-rays, and the treatment administered by College Station Medical Center, there just isn't any additional treatment we can provide to alleviate your son's condition."

Gasping, I was incapable of speaking. He had just delivered a death sentence and I wasn't prepared mentally or emotionally for that news.

"Mr. Williams?"

After a long exhale of hope, I said, "I'm here, Dr. Langford. Are you saying there is nothing more that can be done for our son?"

"His scans show no brain activity and his brain stem is crushed due to the intense swelling. I wish we could offer some alternate treatment, but there simply isn't. There is no recovery from his condition."

"So, you're confirming what the doctors here are saying, that my son is dead."

"Based on the information provided, there is nothing more medically anyone can do."

"We were very hopeful that Methodist Hospital would be the answer to our prayers and that maybe something could be done to save our son. Are you one hundred percent certain?"

"Mr. Williams, I wish I weren't, but yes. I'm one hundred percent certain."

I saw no need to continue the conversation. At that point, our situation was hopeless.

"Thank you for your time, Dr. Langford. Good-bye."

In an instant the air was sucked from the room and, along with it, all hope. The magnitude of that moment was nothing less than heart-stopping. No spiritual or human resource can even come close to preparing a parent for the news that their child is dead.

Not even God.

The magnitude of my heartache struck me much deeper than what my outwardly emotions expressed. As a believer, I have a soul, which is my spiritual embodiment with God. It cried out with profound sorrow. Someday, my mortal body will die, but the gravity of that moment will survive to accompany my heartbroken soul. Relief will only be achieved through my spiritual reunion with my son.

For now, my mind, soul, and spirit begged to know, WHERE IS GOD?

Everyone in the waiting room heard the conversation and they all knew what it meant. The quiet was deafening until I remembered an earlier conversation.

"Aisha mentioned she was working with two additional hospitals in the medical center, just in case this transfer fell through. We should call her now and check that status. Hopefully, she had better luck."

The collective looks from everyone didn't encourage and their defeated body language offered me no hope. Albeit an unlikely possibility, I still retained a slight glimmer of hope. I had to make that call.

Aisha and I exchanged very brief information and the solemn tone of my good-bye gave evidence that the light of hope had extinguished. No hospital was willing to take Nic and we were out of options. Death's claustrophobic walls were closing in around us when Arlene abruptly left the suffocating confines of the waiting room. By instinct, I followed her to the airy corridor of the ICU.

The accumulated stress and the rejected transfer news had finally taken its toll and she broke down.

"Ahhhhrieee!!!"Arlene cried, wailing as loud as her voice could carry. "Ahhhhriee!!!"

Her cry of a mother's anguish was forceful enough to echo through the hallway and the patient's rooms, alerting everyone of death's arrival. She was barely comprehensible, but her words were clear to everyone in the corridor that accepting the news of Nic's fate was a devastating reality no parent should ever endure.

The nurses glanced down the hall in our direction, but returned to their original positions. I suppose the sensitive discretion of allowing families to grieve in their own private way prevented their interference.

At once, I came to her aid, put my arms around her, and secured her with my embrace. With her head pressed against my shoulder, she released the weight of her grief and I struggled to keep us both upright. She sobbed until she reached a point of clarity.

As tears poured from her saturated eyes, she looked at me and screamed in a bloodcurdling voice, "My baby is dead!! He's gone, Greg."

"I know." I paused a few seconds and whispered in her ear, "But God's in control."

Those comforting words were the only ones that came to my mind, but they rang hollow. My faith was shattered. Unconvinced God even cared, my response was more of a cliché reaction than anything. *If God was indeed in control, why was this happening?*

As her cries became more of a whimper, Deborah joined us in the hallway to let us know Tiffany was just spotted in the parking lot. Arlene wasn't bashful about her outpouring of grief, but she didn't want Tiffany to assume the worst when she first walked through the hospital doors. I volunteered to meet her at the entrance and hoped that would give Arlene enough time to gather her emotions.

Without a second to spare, I got there just as Tiffany triggered the motion detector and the glass doors swung open. A spitting image of her mother with only a braided hairdo to differentiate the generations, she's still the most beautiful woman I know. Fathers are allowed such biases.

"Hey, Tootie."

Of the several nicknames she goes by, Tootie is my favorite. Kissing her cheek, I gave a gentle, but reassuring hug.

"Hi, Dad."

While exiting my embrace, I extended a handshake to David. As a strong candidate for my future son-in-law, I kinda like him. No man is ever quite good enough for the scrutinizing eye of a father, but he more than met many of my unrealistic expectations. Aside from the oversized ears, he's a handsome young man with a bright future. When teasing Tiffany about him, I always spoke in hushed tones for fear of him overhearing us.

I extended my hand as I stepped to greet David. "Hey, how was the drive?"

"Hi, Mr. Williams, it was fine. We got here as quickly as we could."

We exchanged handshakes, but our eyes didn't meet. Mine were zeroed in on Tiffany's uncharacteristic glare of concern.

Tiffany brushed passed David and blurted, "Dad, where's Mom?"

"She's in the waiting room along with Deborah,

Leonora, Uncle Dave, Aunt Gert, Aunt Rosa, and several more family members. We'll go there in a few."

Tiffany grabbed my right hand and pulled me closer "Is everything okay?"

I tried my best to conceal my somber tone. "I wish it was, but it's not. We'll explain everything when we get to the waiting room. If you want to go freshen up first, we have a room at the Courtyard Marriott across the freeway."

"No, let's talk first."

"Okay, follow me, sweetheart."

With the corner of her lips cast in a downward frown, Tiffany looked as if she already knew what we were about to tell her. Of course, we planned to be truthful, but we also wanted to encourage hope against all odds. I had to ask myself, *Was hope a reasonable possibility or a futile effort?*

Because of my faith, maintaining a sense of hope is essential. But considering the news of the failed transfer, my faith was placed on life support as well.

Still, I wanted to believe in a miracle.

As we passed the larger waiting room, I pointed to all the students camped there, waiting to see Nic.

Her eyebrows shot up. "Are all of those people Nic's friends?"

"Apparently so. Oh, and by the way, they all refer to him as Nico, so your mother and I have been attempting to use that new nickname when addressing them."

Tiffany stopped abruptly and gave me a twisted

look. "Dad, he's been going by that name for a while now. You guys didn't know about it?"

"I remember him saying something about it, but I didn't know the extent of it." With my hands raised and opened, I was curious. "Do you know how it came about?"

Tiffany smiled with the anticipation of telling her little brother's secret. "Yes, he was playing around with some friends one day and they were trying out lyrics for a rap song. He rapped that Nico was short for Nicotine and everybody knows Nicotine is addictive. So, Nico stuck after that and as they say, the rest is history."

"Huh? Really, I had no idea."

As the older sibling, Tiffany was unapologetic as she declared her position. "Well, Dad, he may wanna be called Nico, but I'm not changing. His nickname will always be Nic for me."

"Me, too, sweetheart, meeee, too."

We reached the waiting room after about ten minutes of delaying Tiffany's arrival on purpose. Upon opening the door, my laser beam eyes focused on Arlene's appearance. A gallon of eye drops couldn't clear the redness from her eyes, but, thank God, she seemed to be okay. She greeted Tiffany and David with hugs and a "don't ask, don't tell" expression.

Of course, the family was aware of the news we had just received and they did a very good job of concealing their emotions. Arlene embraced Tiffany and held on to her for dear life. If she were substituting

Nic for Tiffany, she wasn't about to let him go. I knew exactly how she felt.

Arlene asked everyone to leave the room to give us a little private time with Tiffany before she went to visit her brother. David moved over to join them when Arlene asked him to stay.

"Hey, Little Girl... You okay?" Arlene's voice cracked, accompanied by a distraught look she could no longer conceal.

Tiffany noticed a partially smeared tear in the corner of Arlene's eye and wiped it away. "Yeah, Mom, I'm fine but I can tell you're really upset."

"I can't pretend all is good. It's not. Did you have time to do a little research about bacterial meningitis before you guys left San Antonio?"

"Yes, we did, so I know how dangerous the disease can be. How is he doing?"

"Not well at all, but we're still praying for a miracle. Sit down and I'll give you all the details."

As they sat on the body-battered couch, it provided a level of comfort while yet another tragic story unfolded. Cracks in the leather cushions and the worn body impressions suggested a similar tale had been told thousands of times before. A loved one is somehow injured that led to this destination of hope and despair.

Tiffany hung on every word as Arlene fought to restrain a constant flow of tears. She managed to tell most of the story without breaking down until the part about Nic's arrival at the hospital.

"When he got to the hospital, he went into a coma several minutes after arrival. They suspected bacterial meningitis and confirmed it with a spinal tap fluid test. They've taken several tests and—"

At that point, Arlene's voice quivered and she couldn't continue.

Tiffany stood up to calm her mother by rubbing her shoulder. "Mom, you don't have to explain any further. Dad can finish for you."

"Sure, Tootie."

I filled her in on all the details including the disappointing news about the transfer.

"Since the start, we've been asking everyone and anyone to pray for your brother." With a tight fist, I pounded my chest twice with absolute confidence. "It's going to take a miracle and God is still in the miracle-making business. We're not giving up. If nothing changes after a week, we'll reassess things at that point."

She lowered her hand to the couch as she prepared to sit back down. Her blank stare told me the disturbing news wasn't what she expected. Now, she more than understood why Arlene was so upset and crying at the very thought of Nic's condition. David stepped forward to console her in the same manner she had just moments earlier with her mother.

Tiffany looked up at me. "Do they know how he got it?"

"No. If it's just one case, they won't do an investigation. Some people carry the bacteria in their nose and throat and, for no apparent reason, it sometimes becomes active. They have no idea why."

"When they say no brain activity, is there a chance he can regain it?"

To spare her the pain, I wanted to lie sooo badly, but a lie would only delay and not change the inevitable. "Based on what the doctors are telling us, no, he can't. In essence, they're saying he's brain dead with no possibility of recovery."

She gasped in disbelief. "Dad, no! That can't be true."

"I know, but bacterial meningitis can do tons of damage within just a few hours. That's why we have to continue praying. God is all we have now."

"I need to go see him," she said through a clinched jaw.

"Sure, we can go right now. Arlene, you wanna join us?"

"No, you and Tiffany go ahead and I'll catch up later."

CHAPTER 5

DAY TWO (p.m.)

I hate cold weather. A slight chill in the air to signify a change of seasons is good; but I can do without the ice, snow, and freezing temperatures. Living in the Deep South, I'm rarely exposed to such harsh conditions, but that day was the exception.

When we packed earlier that morning, the weather was the farthest thing from my mind so I had no idea it would turn brutally cold. While we listened to the news reports in the larger waiting room, the public was advised to stay off the roads and highways. Earlier rain had caused the roads to ice over as the temperature dropped. Several friends and relatives wanted to visit, but we advised them to stay home. The last thing we needed was to have someone injured in a car accident on our behalf.

I'm not sure why, but the sudden change of the weather struck me as an omen that Nic's life would not be spared. One had nothing to do with the other, but for some reason I couldn't dismiss the correlation. The weather must have dropped 30 degrees and my reluctant expectations followed the descent. The cloudless gray skies and bone-chilling wind more than convinced me that death was on the horizon.

Nic was dying, yet I believed God would send a message that would sustain my faith. A blistering winter chill was not the message I expected.

We entered Nic's room, where three of his friends visited with him. They were laughing and reminiscing about some party they had all attended several weeks ago. They were doing just as we asked of them earlier and we all hoped for a reaction.

After exchanging introductions, I asked the students to please give Tiffany some time alone with her brother. They complied with tender graciousness, but insisted on coming back later. They had many more stories to share, and the more, the merrier.

When Tiffany saw the respirator hooked up to Nic, she gasped before approaching his bedside. For a brief moment, her fear and faith battled for control of how to approach him.

And then all at once, she said in a stern voice, "Okay, Nic, I'm here now so wake up and get your big butt out of that bed. You have always faked things to get attention, so just stop playing games." She waited a few moments and increased the volume of her command. "Nic, I said I'm here now!!! Nic, I'm here. Please wake up."

With no reaction from Nic, timidity replaced the confidence in her voice. She paused for a moment and nudged his ribs where he had always reacted with laughter. "Please wake up."

When he didn't respond, she turned around and gazed at me with the tears of a desperate child who needs her parent's assurance that everything will be okay. When the realization sank in, she sobbed, "Dad, he's not waking up."

She raised her hands, signaling that she didn't know what else to do. Even at 22 years old, I still viewed her as my baby girl needing daddy to kiss her little boo-boo. After I pulled her into the comfort of my outstretched arms, the wetness from her tears penetrated my shirt.

As much as I wanted to, I wouldn't be the hero she was accustomed to. Her cries ripped to shreds what was left of my damaged heart. Witnessing one child be crushed due to the condition of her sibling was more than I could take. My parental instinct wanted to ease her pain by claiming Nic would get better, but the reality of the moment dictated otherwise. Tiffany had to understand the severity of Nic's situation, so I had no room for sugarcoating it.

If a miracle weren't forthcoming very soon, the unthinkable possibility of Nic's death would become a reality. Tiffany stayed in my nurturing arms for several minutes, but it seemed like hours until she signaled for David to relieve me. They stayed and chatted while I headed back to the waiting room.

Walking down the corridor, I found Gabby and several students talking with an older man with a very thick mustache and wearing a navy blue, pinstriped suit along with a bold red tie and matching handkerchief. With students surrounding him like a rock star, he must have been someone of significance.

I had assumed Gabby and Nic became close friends because of their shared ethnicity. Of the many pictures with his friends, Gabby was the only African American in them. She spoke with a thick southern drawl and often referred to us as "Y'all". Her inviting eyes were indeed a window to her beautiful soul and she welcomed us like she had known us for years.

Gabby waved me over for an introduction. "Hi, Mr. Williams, if you have time I'd like to introduce you to our president, Dr. Loftin."

"Hi, Gabby. Sure."

"Dr. Loftin, this is Nico's dad, Mr. Williams."

He extended his right arm for a firm handshake. "Mr. Williams, I am so sorry about Nico, but please know that he and your family have our full support. Nico is a member of the Aggie family and we offer our full hospitality to you."

"Thank you so much. This is indeed an honor to know you took the time to stop by."

"Aggies stand united with Nico and we pray for his quick recovery. How's he doing?"

"I wish we had some good news, but no one sees improvement with his condition right now. The doctors still say there's no brain activity. But we're not giving up hope."

"Neither will we. I haven't had the pleasure of meeting Nico, but several students I do know have nothing but high praises for him. He's a fine young man and I'm proud to call him an Aggie."

"Thank you, and trust me, Nico adores being an Aggie."

"Here's my card. Please call me if you need assistance with anything and I do mean anything."

"Thank you. Everyone has been so helpful and their support has been a godsend for my family. The students have been amazing and the Critical Incident Response Team even took the liberty to reserve us a hotel room. I honestly cannot say enough about how well we've been treated and it really helps us cope with this tragedy."

We shook hands again and parted ways. I couldn't believe the president of Texas A&M took the time to visit. With a student population of over 48,000, he has a lot on his plate and making that effort reinforced my new perspective about the institution. His gesture said a lot about him and the university he administers.

Once again, I was impressed with the whole Aggie spirit thing. Their dedication and compassion for one another is a commendable characteristic I increasingly admired. I felt extremely happy for Nic to be a member of the Aggie Family.

I dreaded going back to talk with Arlene and our families about the next plan of action. I had no clue of what that possibility could be. I didn't expect to find her all alone in the room. With the weather turning so bad and the roads just as dangerous, the darkness added yet another element that could potentially threaten our family's safe return.

"Is everyone gone now?" I said.

"Yes, they will come back tomorrow, but I discouraged them. There's no point in their risking their lives driving back here, particularly if there's no change in Nic's condition."

"Yeah, I agree. The weather is freezing and it's just too risky with the icy roads. Hey, right before I came in, Gabby introduced me to A&M's president, Dr. Loftin. He was here to check on Nic. Can you believe that?"

Arlene's eyes popped open. She looked as surprised as I did. "Noooo, Are you serious? The president of the university?"

"Yep, I swear it was him. Taking the time to visit us speaks volumes about him, this university, and the Aggie Spirit we hear so much about." I don't think I could have smiled any broader. "This place is so impressive. Now it's easy to see why Nic loves it so much. Never in my wildest dreams did I ever think A&M was such a welcoming and supportive institution for African Americans. This is a significant paradigm shift for me."

"I feel exactly the same. I'm just amazed at how caring and encouraging they all are." Arlene pointed to some items on the coffee table and described in detail how helpful Nic's friends had been. "Gabby was in here along with some others and they kept bringing us coffee and snacks to eat. I tried sending them away to rest, but they always refused."

"Nic is so blessed to have such caring friends. They don't know us from Adam, yet they're treating us like we've been part of their immediate families. Thank God for each and every one of them. If we didn't have their support, I honestly don't know how we could cope with all that has happened. They give me strength."

I nodded. "How is Tiffany?"

"My heart broke watching her attempt to awaken Nic. That moment will stay with me till my dying day. She approached him with contempt like she always does. She condemned him for doing all of this for attention and now that she's here, he can surely stop faking and wake up. She repeated, wake up Nic, several times before she realized her efforts were hopeless. She turned, fell in my arms, and we both started crying."

Arlene put down a half-eaten Snickers and approached the door in haste. "My poor baby. I need to go be with her." She brushed pass me in a rush to the door, but I stopped her.

"David is with her now. She's okay for the time being."

"We have to pay really close attention to her. She acts all tough, but you know it's all an act, right?" Arlene gave me half a smile.

"Ohhhhhh yes, I'm well aware of her acting skills."

"I hate to admit it, but she's hoodwinked me a few times."

Silence settled like a cloud between us for a moment.

"Ya know, Arlene, maybe I should go to Walmart and buy us a couple sweaters. Not sure how long this cold spell will last, but we could use a jacket or something."

"Good idea. I didn't pack any winter clothes. What about Tif? Did she bring any?"

"Yes, she brought her coat, so she's good to go. I better leave now before the weather gets worse. See you in a bit."

"Be careful, Greg. The news reports say the roads are really dangerous out there."

"Whaaaat???? You're actually concerned about my safety. I thought you would probably want me to drive super-fast and let the chips fall where they may."

"Oh, trust me, I do. I'm still paying life insurance on your butt and I'm the sole beneficiary, so, please, drive like a bat outta hell!"

We both managed to force out gentle smiles, but only for a second or two. The weight of the day's disappointment didn't leave much room for laughter. In spite of everything, enjoying a little humor felt refreshing.

Although the store was only two or three miles from the hospital, it felt like hours passed before reaching my destination. The drive was tedious and slow, a welcoming distraction. Anything was better than focusing on the consequences of Methodist

Hospital's rejection. During the brief time away, a vast surge of questions about my withering faith invaded my defenseless mind.

Why hasn't God given us any signs of hope? If this was a test of my faith, how much was I to endure?

Why didn't we know about the meningitis threat? Why didn't the clinic accurately diagnose Nic? How do I respond if the doctors tell me conclusively that he died?

Why hasn't God responded?

Wave after wave of emotions crashed on the shores of my mind and the erosion of my faith was unavoidable. All that remained was an undercurrent of hopelessness that begged the question: *Why?*

I RETURNED TO THE HOSPITAL without incident and found Arlene visiting with a couple of Nic's friends, two well-groomed and personable young men. They introduced themselves as Bret and Cliff and they had stories to tell about their wild adventures with Nico.

Every so often, Arlene and I glanced at each other with amazement because we didn't recognize the guy they kept referring to as Nico. He did rap songs, was the life of the party, danced boldly in public, played practical jokes, and was this hugely popular guy everyone wanted to hang around.

Bret gave us a little insight into the jokester Nic had become. "Nico had nicknames for many of his friends and mine was C Minus."

"Why C Minus?" I said.

"Nico told me girls have a rating scale when it comes to men. Obviously he was an A plus, so in comparison to him, I couldn't possibly be any higher than a C Minus. The name stuck and it's now my official nickname."

Hearing all those wonderful and humorous stories about Nic opened my eyes to the young man our son had morphed into and I couldn't be more excited for him. All those frustrating years of exclusion and hurt feelings were forever behind him. His future was indeed bright and the world at his fingertips, but now, I questioned whether fate would afford him the opportunity.

Because of Texas A&M, the Aggie Spirit or whatever Aggie influence it was, the Nico persona was unleashed and life would never be the same for him. As difficult as the day had been, I was convinced that Nic's new found confidence was even more reason to believe God would answer our prayers. Surely God would save him and allow the miracle to be a testament from a gifted young man whose developing confidence knew no bounds.

☆ ☆ ☆

THE EVENING WAS GETTING late, so Arlene urged the boys to go visit their buddy. Again, we encouraged them to talk about all their crazy times together from the very moment they met him. We wanted them to laugh, joke, and reminisce with him while we prayed he could hear something that would prompt an emotional or physical response.

At that point, anything he could do voluntarily would be a significant contradiction to what the doctors were telling us. We would accept any news. A flicker of his eyelid would be a monumental improvement and confirmation that God's pending miracle had begun.

Holding on to my faith was as difficult as trying to hold water in my fist, yet I still believed God was much bigger than the challenges we faced.

The boys gave us both hugs and words of encouragement before they left to visit their bud. Arlene and I at last had an opportunity to discuss our next plan of action, if indeed there was one.

I repositioned one of the chairs the boys had occupied and sat down in front of Arlene. "So, where do we go from here? After the rejection by the hospitals, I don't think trying to get Nic transferred is an option any longer."

"I agree, but I don't know where to look for answers. I just knew deep in my soul that Methodist Hospital would accept him."

"Yeah, me, too. Well, we still have to keep our faith in God that he will deliver. When man cannot do, God can."

"I have faith, Greg. I hope you know that." The space between her eyebrows narrowed and suggested a bit of uncertainty.

"Oh, of course I know that."

"I will be honest with you, though. I believe it could be God's will not to save Nic."

"Why do you believe that?"

"I can't even begin to understand God's reasoning or logic, but if he elects not to act, we have to accept it."

"Obviously, we have to accept whatever Nic's fate will be, but why do you believe what you believe?" Baffled, I sat back, grabbed the chair's armrest and listened to Arlene's flawed logic with the same confusion as Dr. Cunningham's diagnosis.

"After receiving the news today, I thought it's just not meant to be, for whatever reason. People pray every day for this and for that, and many times those prayers go unanswered."

In frustration, I pounded the armrest with both fists. "Yes, but for every prayer that is not answered, many, many more are."

"Trust me, Greg, I'm not giving up hope, but we have to open ourselves up to the possibility that Nic is gone."

For a brief second, the woman sitting before me appeared to be a complete stranger. I took a long pause and exhaled a deep breath of discontentment. "Just can't do it. When visiting with him, I see flashbacks of his entire life. From the day he was born until last month when we went to church together. He still has a future, a life to live, a wife to marry, and children to raise, so giving up is not an option. I will pray and continue to pray until he gets better. At this point, that's all we have."

"I'm right there with you, Greg, but you should also pray that we recognize any sign from God that tells us his plan. It could be that he will heal Nic or call him home."

Not daring to verbalize my thoughts, I had assumed we were on the same page. Was she actually suggesting we look for a reason to accept Nic's death? How could she even consider the possibility? Had she given up hope?

Before responding, I remembered working at the church as a lay counselor many years ago and studying the five stages of grief: Denial, Anger, Bargaining, Depression, and Acceptance. After Methodist Hospital's rejection, she leapfrogged to the fifth stage of Acceptance.

Since the very moment I received the news about Nic, my complete trust was with God. When negative thoughts entered my mind, I prayed for strength to hold on to God's Word.

Isn't that the whole purpose of faith?

This is our son, our baby, and we should never, ever give up hope. The moment "Acceptance" creeps into our consciousness, we may as well start planning a funeral.

As events had developed during the past two days, I experienced the first four stages of grief. And my faith was stretched to its limit, but Acceptance was still an eternity away for me. Conventional medical treatment had run its course, and even with heavy odds stacked against any sort of recovery, I maintained my optimism.

"Arlene, I hear you, but I can't—"

She sprang up from the couch and unloaded her tirade. "GREG, JUST STOP AND LISTEN TO ME!" As her suppressed road-rage frustration was unleashed, the one vein in the middle of her forehead tripled in size.

She glared at me, and then her expression thawed one degree. "There is nothing more I want more than to see Nic fully recover and live out the remainder of his life. All I am saying is that our prayer should also include that we are open-minded enough to receive God's message, whatever that may be and not just what we want to hear."

The rage returned, as she held up her palm to silence me. "IS THAT ASKING TOO DAMN MUCH?"

I knew as sure as I loved my son, she was dead on right. Even though she made a valid point, my automatic self-defense response shouted right back. Pushing the chair backwards, I stood with just inches separating us. "I can understand that God could possibly have other plans, but for the life of me, I can't believe those plans would involve Nic's death." I shouted with the same level of frustration hurled at me. "What purpose would it serve? WHY WON'T GOD JUST SPEAK ALOUD?"

I shuddered and stepped away from her. "NOW, IS THAT TOO DAMN MUCH TO ASK?"

We glanced at one another without saying a word. I didn't want things to escalate any further so I paused, buried my head in my hands, and took a long deep breath. "I just don't know any more, Arlene. I'll give some thought to what you said, but for now, I'm going visit with Nic. You wanna join me or sit here while we continue screaming at each other?"

"No, Greg, I don't want to argue anymore, but I need you to see the bigger picture." She paused. "Ya know what, just forget it. I have some calls to make and I'll join you when I'm done."

"Okay. Where's Tiffany and David?"

"They stopped by earlier and decided to go rest a bit at the hotel. Before leaving, Tiffany gave an interview to that television news crew we saw earlier."

"Really? Are they still around?"

"Yep, apparently Nic's situation is becoming a newsworthy story."

"I just wish he'd wake up. NOW, that would be a news story worthy of broadcasting to the whole world. The headlines would read, Young Man Given Up for Dead Miraculously Makes a Full Recovery. If only God was willing."

Time flew by and it was already half past 10 p.m.

I hadn't noticed the shift change or the quietness the late night brings as the hustle of the day vanished into the darkness. The stillness of nighttime almost makes one believe agony takes an eight-hour break.

Was Arlene's suggestion the right one? Should I also consider the constant "no change in his condition" as a message from God? Bewildered, I lowered my head and leaned against the vacant corridor wall pleading with God, *Why? Why not do something to give us just a tiny drop of hope?*

After my brief appeal, I resumed my way towards Nic's room and was astonished at the sight. A group of Nic's friends surrounded his bed, reading scriptures for him. Again, those young people who with such affection call themselves Aggies blew me away by their love and commitment. They could have been at dozens of places, involved in all sorts of activities, yet they chose to spend their time praying for their ailing friend. I found it impossible to think any more highly of them.

At every turn, I felt overwhelmed with emotion, either from the lack of improvement or from the love exhibited by everyone who heard the news. Coping with the range of emotions from appreciation to desperation, and back to appreciation again exhausted me.

Tiptoeing into the room, I tried not to disturb their concentration, but they acknowledged me and invited me to join them. Cliff, one of the young men who had visited us earlier that evening, led the prayer vigil. Altogether, there were about six students, four guys and two girls praying. They prayed with the same determination and expectancy from God as I did. I believed surely God would hear and answer the prayers of those young followers of his Word.

While joining in, my eyes were closed and my head lowered in reverence to God. As Cliff continued, "Father, we gather here to humbly—"

"Did anyone see that?" one student hissed.

"See what?" said another student. "My eyes were shut."

"Nico moved his toe. I saw his big toe twitch."

Considering the diagnosis, I thought it a shocking statement and one we all wanted to witness with our own eyes. Although I stood right next to the young man, like everyone else, I didn't see a thing. Because of his convincing assertion, we all focused on Nic's toe with the anticipation he would move it again.

Maybe, just maybe, that tiny drop of hope I prayed for minutes earlier was now being answered. My eyes became a microscope zeroing in on the one body part Nic might be capable to move.

Excited to the extreme and pumped with soooo much adrenaline, I wanted to run down the halls and scream, THANK YOU, JESUS!!!

Needing to see the evidence with my own eyes first was probably best, so I postponed my declaration. While we stared and waited, I wanted Arlene and Tiffany to witness God's miracle, but again, waiting for confirmation was best.

As we focused on Nic's toe, the thought of confronting Dr. Cunningham, Dr. Okafor, and all the naysayers was just so tempting. I couldn't wait to tell them all, SEE, TOLD YOU SO! Instead of getting the consistent "there is no brain activity and there is no change in his condition," I expected to hear them proclaim with profound confusion, "We can't explain it, but he's improving."

They couldn't explain it, but I sure could. Nothing is impossible with God, and the simple, but monumental, movement of Nic's toe would soon acknowledge my trust and faith in him.

Minutes passed and nothing happened. The prayers continued and intensified with the expectation of God's intervention.

My heart beat with the same anticipation at Nic's birth. Scared of the unpredictability, but assured all would be fine.

We prayed, we stared, and we waited. After about an hour or so with no movement, my sky-high enthusiasm started its descent. No one questioned the young man about what he claimed he saw and God knows we all wanted to believe him.

Not being aware of how long the group had been praying prior to my appearance, I'm sure fatigue may have played a role in what he thought he saw. Disheartened after a couple hours and nervous waiting for any type of movement, I decided to leave. Physical exhaustion and a huge drain from the latest emotional roller coaster ride made rest my evasive recourse. With no reason to believe God's miracle was imminent, I headed back to tell Arlene what happened.

Unfazed by my encounter, Arlene only wanted to know if my prayer was now modified. On the surface, yes, but privately, my soul held out for the tiniest mustard seed of hope.

The sunrise was a few hours away and joining it would be the dreaded possibility of Stage 5. The hourglass of Nic's life was down to a few grains of sand and, without God's immediate intervention, time was about to run out.

While driving to our hotel, I pondered the question of God's absence, which remained an ever-present mystery.

CHAPTER 6

DAY THREE

The thick curtains of our hotel room offered little resistance to the sunlight illuminating their edges. Designed to keep the morning light from disturbing my sleep, the curtains were no more effective than my faith in convincing me of my son's recovery.

Sluggish from only one hour of sleep, I did a double take at the alarm clock and suspected some sort of malfunction. Five hours had passed and it was time to face another hellish day of more negative reports. Hoping our prayers were answered while we slept, I wondered if the day would be the first of many to praise and celebrate Nic's return.

In either scenario, God was in control and my complete but dwindling trust was with him.

While everyone was still asleep, I prayed, "God, please heal Nic and bring him back to us. But, if that's not your plan, your will be done. We also ask that you provide us a sign or the ability to recognize your intent. In Jesus name, Amen."

Arlene overheard me and she thanked me for amending my prayer.

Next, Tiffany stirred as well. "Mom, what are you thanking Dad for?"

"I asked him to pray for clarity about God's will regarding your brother. Of course, we all want and pray that he recovers, but that may not be God's will."

Tiffany gave the same confused look at Arlene as I did earlier, so I jumped in to provide some explanation. "Your mother is right in that we don't know God's will, so she asked me to modify my prayer for his will to be revealed. That does not mean we stop praying for Nic's full recovery, because I won't."

Sitting up, Tiffany appeared alerted as she faced my direction. "Dad, but what if there continues to be no change in Nic's condition?"

"Well, I will interpret that to mean we keep praying and don't give up. We're not doing anything for a least a week of Nic being in the hospital. Things look pretty bleak right now, but things can turn around at any second. And, you and David need to do the same."

"Of course, Dad, but—"

Sitting up and turning to face her, I spoke to her in a firm but loving tone. "Tootie, there's no room for buts right now. We will face whatever we have to when the time comes. Okay?"

"Okay, Dad," she said, bowing her head while appearing defiant to my position.

Having just got out of bed, I addressed everyone.

"Since everybody seems to be up now, let's all go have breakfast before we head over to the hospital."

Arlene called to check the status, and again, no change reported. Hardly any conversation took place during breakfast and the mood was solemn. The sounds of utensils scraping against plates while scooping up food was more preferable than discussing the obvious. We avoided eye contact to prevent each other from seeing the truth behind our forced optimism. While trying to remain hopeful, I found it increasing difficult to push back any negative thoughts of "Acceptance."

Although still freezing, the weather had improved to a warmer degree overnight. We arrived at the hospital around 7:30 and some of Nic's friends were already seated in the waiting room. We stopped by a minute or two to say good morning and to give them the same ole hopeless message "no change at this point."

When so much expectation is met with absolute repudiation, the fate of hopelessness invades every thought. Although worried, I passionately believed in my most trusted scripture:

Trust in the LORD with all your heart; and lean not unto your own understanding. In all your ways acknowledge him, and he will make your paths straight.

Proverbs 3:5-6

That one scripture had always been my favorite and now I needed to believe in it more than at any other time in my life. Afraid of facing more bad news from the doctors, I needed the scripture to bring me a certain level of comfort and confidence. By completely trusting God and stop trying to understand the whys and the hows, then, just maybe, I could get through the ordeal without losing my mind.

In parting, we encouraged Nic's friends to continue praying for him and not to give up hope. He was a fighter and we needed them to fight just as hard.

Little did they know how their presence alone gave us strength to cope with whatever we would face that day. Having never been in a situation like that before, I can't imagine how difficult it must be without the support of so many people. You expect your family to be there, but the Aggie Spirit was relentless! We left the waiting room encouraged by their optimism, but guarded by fate's reality.

As we walked into Nic's room together, our family bond transcended the divorce and all the pain associated with it. We were a united family filled with love for one another and determined to support each other through the term of discontent.

Tiffany spoke first, "Good morning, Nic. We're baaaaack."

Arlene and I smiled at Tiffany mimicking a scene from the movie, *Poltergeist*. Her attempt at joking with him was heartwarming and brought back so many fond memories. He was notorious for being frightened of any movie that had scary scenes in it. He and I had seen the movie, *Snakes on a Plane*, and he did something that had me rolling out of my seat with laughter.

I'm terrified of snakes and I'll do whatever to avoid them. In this instance, a movie gave me no reason to fear anything. Many unexpected scenes caused the audience to gasp or, in some cases, scream with fear. In one particular scene, a large anaconda wrapped itself around one of the passengers and was about to devour its victim when I turned to see how Nic was reacting.

To my surprise, he was sitting Indian-style in his seat with his head down, avoiding the movie and any snakes that could be near his feet.

Trying to contain myself, I couldn't help but burst out laughing!! He had looked up, smiled, and said with confidence, "That snake won't get me."

Arlene greeted him with her pet name, "Good morning, Little Man! It's time you wake up today and show some signs of getting out of that bed."

She pulled up a chair and chatted with him about all his friends who had come by to visit. She repeated all the humorous stories told to her and about how much he means to them. Tiffany had lots of stories to tell about their growing up as siblings. She threatened to reveal his deepest secrets if he didn't wake up soon. Of course, she was only teasing, but if it somehow triggered a response, she would have continued without hesitation. I appreciated David's effort of chipping in, even though he didn't have an extensive relationship with Nic.

To my surprise, I didn't have much to say during the visit. Hearing their stories created a nostalgic moment and presented an opportunity to reflect on our lives together. Watching Arlene and Tiffany talk with Nic took me back to a period when he was about five years old and we had gone on a Sea World family vacation.

We experienced what we thought at the time was a parent's worst nightmare. Nic got separated from us after a Shamu act ended. We were all walking together when all of a sudden he was nowhere to be found. After we searched at a frantic pace for several minutes, other people joined our panic state and screamed his name, NIIIIICCCCC!! NIIIIICCCCC!!

We had just drawn the attention of a policeman when Tiffany pointed him out at a waterfall playground for children. Nic was running from one water feature to the next, getting soaked. Seeing him laughing and having so much fun, Tiffany had joined her little brother and they enjoyed the time of their lives.

I suspected God now sent that memory to assure me that our worse fears hadn't materialized then and the same would be true for our current situation. Encouraged by that memory, I did my best to deny the constant doubts and fears.

The weather was still cold but warming enough to allow safe travel for anyone who wanted to drive in from Houston. Our families desired to come support us again and we welcomed their visits.

My goddaughter, Falanda Limar, had been eager to come by the day before, but I persuaded her to wait until the weather cleared up. When I called to give an update, she was already on the way and would arrive sometime around noon. Since she is a physician and one of the few people I trust unconditionally, we needed her by our side when speaking with the doctors. Her professional opinion of Nic's situation meant more to me than any specialist offered by the hospital.

My role as godfather hadn't come the routine route by way of Falanda's birth. Her mother Linda, who worked with me at a local school district, introduced her to me as a middle school student. Since her biological father lived out of state, which hampered their relationship, we somehow bonded and our connection developed to the extent that I designated myself as her godfather. With ease, she adapted to becoming a member of our family and the monsters considered her their older sibling.

One of the happiest moments of my life was watching her graduate from medical school and achieving the goals she set from so many years earlier. Of the many attributes I admire about her, the one that shines above all others is her commitment to God. She will do nothing without first praying in earnest about it and then waiting until God provides an answer.

Over the years, I have watched in awe as God's

favor followed her every step of her life. In many ways, our relationship is truly ironic. As the self-appointed godfather, my role included preparing her for life's challenges, but instead she taught me how to trust God to fulfill the desires of my heart. She is indeed a true blessing to my life.

A couple of hours passed and the waiting room was filled to capacity once again. Nic's faithful friends showed up again in support of him and for us as well. We went in to greet and to inform them of the 'still no change in his condition,' but we wanted them to continue praying regardless. I was so inspired by their commitment and their devotion, knowing they were missing classes. Aggie Spirit, there's simply no comparison!

After addressing the students, we proceeded to the waiting room, where our families were preparing for the day's drama. While waiting, we had an unexpected visit from Dr. Cunningham. Every time we met with him, he had offered no encouraging news, and from all appearances, things had gotten progressively worse.

He entered the room accompanied by three additional doctors, all expressing a look of major concern. Whatever discouraging news they were about to dump on us, I assumed they thought the message would be much more convincing if multiple doctors delivered it.

"Good morning, Mr. and Mrs. Williams."

"Good morning, Dr. Cunningham."

"If you have some time, we would like to speak with you about your son's condition. I've invited these specialists to join me, should you have questions that you may feel comfortable asking another doctor. You met Dr. Newsome the other night and, if you recall, he is a neurologist. I've asked another neurologist, Dr. Wright, to review the tests as well, and lastly, I have asked Dr. Bullard, an infectious disease specialist, to review the treatment administered to your son."

We greeted the other doctors; however, before Dr. Cunningham began his consultation, I was compelled to ask a question. "We've been checking Nic's condition with the nurse's station almost every hour and the response is always the same, there's no change. So, before you begin, I'd like to know: Is your message more of the same?"

They might have interpreted my question as cynical, but my patience had run out and I couldn't take hearing any more bad news. It was not his fault, but there were no other options to channel my frustrations.

"Mr. Williams, I wish there was better news, but there is none. Your son's condition is worsening. Additional tests and brain scans have been performed and they do not reveal any change in his condition. Again, there is still no brain activity and no chance of recovery from his current state."

"Okay, you've told us all this before, so how has his situation worsened?"

"His heart is not pumping blood sufficiently to his extremities. In a matter of days, parts of his body, like his fingers, nose, and toes will begin to rot away. Please, trust me when I say you don't want to see that happen. We, as your son's medical team, recommend discontinuing life support before his body begins to decompose."

Standing by my side, Arlene seized my hand and whispered, "Greg, that's the sign we prayed for."

Not for me. I wasn't ready to concede anything until every option available was considered. Turning back to Dr. Cunningham, I said, "Is there any treatment that could increase the blood flow to his extremities?"

Hopeless, he shook his head. "Mr. Williams, may I speak with you privately for a moment?"

After a long sigh, I said, "Sure."

Only he and I stepped just outside the waiting room door and he proceeded to make his plea. "I cannot begin to imagine what you're going through right now and it's very obvious you love your son. If there were anything more we could do, I would move heaven and hell to do it. But there simply is nothing more to be done and that's the same reason why Methodist Hospital rejected the transfer. There isn't anything anyone can do for him now. If you don't mind, I want to share a personal story with you."

I was tempted to roll my eyes in disapproval, but I restrained myself and accepted. "Uh hum."

"I have a brother who lost his daughter about six

months ago and he was faced with a situation very similar to yours. My niece was the victim of a car accident and my brother had to decide whether to continue or stop life support for his daughter. She was gone, but he couldn't tolerate the thought of not giving her every opportunity to recover."

Dr. Cunningham stared into the distance, as if conjuring an image of her. "It was the hardest decision he ever had to make and, as his brother, I begged him to let her go. I didn't want the last image of his pride and joy to be of her body deteriorating before his eyes. After much soul searching, he took my advice and discontinued life support."

He put his hand on my arm. "You're in the exact same situation and there isn't much time before your son's body will start the decomposition process. It's a horrific sight and trust me when I say, you do not want to see that."

I listened with intensity and he was sincere, but trust in him evaded me. I had no reason to question his knowledge or authenticity, but my faith and my optimism wouldn't allow me to concede just yet.

"Thank you, doctor. I really do appreciate your taking the time to share your personal story, and you're right, it's a very difficult decision to make. At any second, my son could show some sign he's still with us and I just can't take away that opportunity. Give us a little time and we will get back to you."

"Sure, but please don't wait too long."

As I opened the door to re-enter the waiting

room, the remaining doctors exited to rejoin Dr. Cunningham. They departed with the same stoic stares of concern of which they entered the room.

Before we could discuss the latest bombshell, the door opened again a split second after the doctors left the room. For a moment, I thought they must have forgotten to tell us something.

But Falanda came in and her timing couldn't have been more precise! I looked at her as God's personal angel sent with the special purpose of setting those doctors straight and to encourage us to keep believing. Throughout the years, I had a first row seat and witnessed too many times how God answered her prayers. Knowing she was praying for Nic's recovery, I was convinced God would respond likewise again.

Like the monsters, she has a pet name as well. She still smiles when I call her, "Spotlight," referencing the bulb shape of her forehead. She denies my exaggeration, but we get a huge laugh when I point out the hairstyle she often uses to camouflage the "spotlight."

After we exchanged hugs and greetings, we gave her the details of what the doctors had just told us. I also explained my reasons for not complying with their recommendation of discontinuing life support. Lastly, Arlene described our modified prayer and how the news just received from the doctor as God's response.

Such information was a lot to drop on her after just arriving, but she needed to meet Dr. Cunningham right away and then advise us. Terrified with fear, I determined to trust whatever news she presented.

By luck, Dr. Cunningham and one of his associates were still in the main corridor just outside the waiting room. I approached him and introduced Falanda as Dr. Limar, who's also my goddaughter. "Dr. Cunningham, if you have a little time, would you please go over all the details of Nic's condition? I've given Dr. Limar my version, but I would feel more comfortable if she received the information directly from you."

"I don't mind at all, but if you want to see the test results, we'll have to go visit with Dr. Newsome."

Dr. Cunningham's eyes sparkled and jumped with the opportunity to share his story. He started from the very beginning when Nic first arrived to the emergency room and I was glad he did. Falanda needed every bit of information available so she could have a comprehensive picture when we talked afterwards.

"Dr. Limar, Nicolis was admitted to our emergency room two days ago. He was noticeably incoherent and..."

My mind drifted as Dr. Cunningham recounted my living nightmare. The loud banging sounds in my head prevented me from hearing a word the doctor said.

Bam... Bam... Bam... became louder with each pounding. The fifth stage of "Acceptance" was beating on the door of my mind with the force of a sledgehammer. Faith's door was holding its own, but it was clear, if a supernatural reinforcement weren't immediate, the door would soon be obliterated.

After about thirty minutes, Dr. Cunningham said, "That's it, Dr. Limar. That's the whole story. If a decision is not reached soon, decomposition of his extremities will begin."

Falanda's body language didn't show any signs of disagreement and she didn't ask any questions that contradicted his conclusions. I was expecting a litany of insinuating questions that would cause Dr. Cunningham to think he was back in medical school.

None were forthcoming. She thanked him for taking the time to explain things in detail and I did as well. Reaching for my hand and looking eye to eye, she didn't say a word. She maintained a straight face, stroked my hand and turned to walk us back to the waiting room.

Bam, once more!

Her silence was the final blow. Its impact shattered faith's door to pieces and "Acceptance" made its grand entrance.

The time arrived for a family meeting and I viewed Falanda as Nic's representative. Everything that had occurred during the past couple of days came down to a moment of truth. Either all of our hopes and prayers would be answered or our worst fears would come to fruition.

Wanting to pray one more time before Falanda spoke, I chose not to. If God were going to save my son, more than enough prayers had already reached their intended destination.

I started the discussion. "Falanda just spoke with Dr. Cunningham and he gave her all the details about Nic's condition. He started from the very beginning and ended by explaining what he told us right before Falanda arrived. I wanted Falanda to speak with Dr. Cunningham because I trust her professionally. The doctors wouldn't lie to us on purpose, but every available option should be considered, regardless of how remote the possibility. And, since she's a doctor, I trust Falanda to know. Does anyone have any questions before she begins?"

Arlene and Tiffany both shook their heads.

I turned to Falanda. "Okay, you have the floor."

Falanda cleared her throat and balanced her medical training approach with her love of us. "I hope you know how much you all mean to me. For years, you've been a second family to me and I can't thank you enough for being a part of my life. When Greg called Tuesday evening to tell me what happened, I didn't believe what he said. Because Nic is always smiling and such a joy to be around, I just couldn't get my head around it. After the conversation ended, I immediately called my mother and we started praying. And, we haven't stopped. Nic is like my little brother and…"

Overwhelmed with emotion, she couldn't finish, so Arlene stepped in for her. "It's okay, we've all had our moments and we will continue to have them.

Please take your time. There's no rush."

Arlene and Tiffany hugged her with an abundance of affection and it helped her cope with what she needed to tell us. After a few minutes, she wiped away the tears, gathered herself and started again.

"God is in control. Whatever the outcome, God is in control."

Arlene murmured, "Yes, he is."

Falanda continued, "After praying with my mom, I researched the diagnosis and treatment. You know all the details by now, so I'll just get straight to what I discussed with Dr. Cunningham. The bacteria circulated throughout Nic's brain and caused intense swelling. As a consequence, the intense swelling crushed his brain stem. Having not reviewed the scans or other tests, I can't confirm everything just yet. If the tests are conclusive, then medically speaking, there is nothing more to be done."

Desperately holding on for any sign of hope, I said, "What about the problem of Nic's extremities not receiving enough blood circulation? Can anything be done to treat that condition?"

Falanda's expression made it crystal clear she wanted to give me something to hope for, anything to hold on to, but there wasn't a thing medically she could offer. Again, she concurred with Dr. Cunningham and hesitated before she said, "No."

With "Acceptance" clearly establishing its occupancy, I just had one last question.

"Is he dead?"

After a long deep sigh, her head slightly bowed and tears dropping from her cheeks, her response was barely audible and yet unmistakable. "Yes."

The room fell silent. Our beloved son and Tiffany's annoying little brother was gone. The fifth stage of Acceptance now overpowered all barriers I had fought so hard to maintain. Now, faithless and hopeless, I abandoned all belief that Nic could be healed.

Nicolis Terrel Williams died.

Lowering my head in my hands, I cried and cried for my child. Not a single parent ever believes their child will precede them in death and I was no different. People die every minute of each day, but no one expects it of their child. Why did God abandon Nic?

Accepting the news felt like an unimaginable illusion and although the possibility was always there, my misguided faith wouldn't allow me to accept it. The magnitude of the moment brought my heart to a standstill. It beat to circulate blood through my body, but it no longer functioned as the center of my emotional being. My body was present, but in mind and feelings, I was a million miles away.

My baby was dead and his once radiant smile would be no more.

God had abandoned us, if he was even there in the first place. I had never prayed with so much determination for anything in my life, and hundreds, if not thousands, of others prayed as well. My faith led me to believe that when two or more pray, God listens and responds.

So, why not this time? What did we do wrong?

Even though the reality of death lurked, waiting to crush my faith, I had believed with deep conviction all our efforts would be rewarded.

> THE DEATH OF ONE'S CHILD IS UNEQUIVOCALLY THE MOST DEVASTATING OF ALL HUMAN EXPERIENCES.
> THE INTENSITY OF PAIN IS BEYOND DESCRIPTION AND UNMATCHED BY ALL HUMAN EMOTION.

Minutes passed without anyone uttering a sound. Accepting the finite truth of Falanda's confirmation bridged the gap between ambiguity and reality. Although the unthinkable was hinted to us many times before, no one had ever used the terms of "death," "died," or "passed on" when describing Nic's condition. The doctors had chosen ambiguous terms like "no brain activity" or "he can't recover."

Right or wrong, I had allowed that ambiguity to create an unrealistic optimism, an idealistic hope.

Arlene whispered to me, "Greg, we prayed for a sign and we prayed for the ability to accept God's will, whatever that may be."

"Yes, we did, but is this really God's will? Why didn't God heal him?"

"You know only God can answer that and that's why we prayed for acceptance, regardless of whatever outcome we would face. We can't question why, but we can be thankful for the gift of having Nic for twenty years."

Arlene was right, but my instinct wanted to continue the fight, despite the insurmountable odds.

She whispered to me as only a loving mother could. "Greg, we gotta let him go."

Tiffany heard her mother and responded with her own plea to keep fighting. "Dad, you said earlier that no decisions would be made for at least a week. Can we still wait until then?"

"I know, Tootie, but things have changed considerably. If it weren't for the news we got this morning, I would hold firm with the decision. There is no chance he will get better and with his extremities starting to decompose, we have to accept it, no matter how much we wanna believe otherwise. He's gone, baby, and we need to prepare for the next steps."

Next steps? And, just what the hell are they?

My arcade ball thoughts were erratic, bouncing from anger to hurt, to betrayal, and then to disillusionment. Yet somehow, I needed to push all that aside and set an agenda for the "next steps." Prayers for strength and wisdom were essential for us to move forward.

But now, prayer for me was an imaginary thought without substance. After conceding to "Acceptance," a tidal wave of "Anger" rushed in. Prayer, faith, and God were no more than fairy tales designed to provide support and a false sense of security for humanity's need to live in blissful eternity.

Arlene sensed my immediate mood change and suggested Tiffany go visit with Nic's friends to give us an opportunity to talk privately. Our daughter seemed to be in a very fragile state of mind and we didn't want her to hear us discuss the morbid details of planning a funeral or organ donation.

I would have given anything to join her. The subjects of a burial, a funeral, and organ donation were just as foreign as speaking Chinese to me, yet we quickly received a crash course from several family members and from Arlene's church. Falanda stayed and helped us plan all the forbidden activities no parent should ever have to tackle.

With so many inquiries about Nic's condition, the first order of business was to send out a prepared statement informing everyone about his status. It had to be worded just right without necessarily announcing his death. Officially, he hadn't died, but the statement could not suggest there was still hope. News reporters were calling, A&M was asking questions along with hundreds of family members and friends. We assigned that task to Falanda, while we discussed organ donation and what type of burial service.

I was shocked to find we agreed without much debate. We figured Nic would want his organs donated, even though he didn't specify as such on his driver's license. As much as he loved people, we knew he would want to help others.

That decision was easy. Deciding on a traditional

burial versus cremation could have been a significant disagreement, but not this time. I suggested cremation and Arlene agreed without hesitation. I had expected an opposing view, but thank God she agreed and we avoided an argument.

We left Falanda to speak with Dr. Cunningham regarding our decision to disconnect life support. The next order of business was to speak with the organ donation people. Their earlier attempt was met with a very hostile response and rightly so. But now, no question or debate lingered about Nic's health status. We scheduled the appointment for the next morning.

After the brief meeting, I took a moment to comprehend the magnitude of what we just agreed to, the decisions we made, and the ones still awaiting our attention. My emotions were dehydrated and my spirit paralyzed after accepting the realization that Nic was dead.

On purpose I chose not to use the more accepted term, "passed away." Society embraces the term because it's an easier substitute for our minds to accept. An unexpected death brings unimaginable pain and I wanted others to feel the reality of the term with its greatest impact.

Upon returning to the waiting room, I found my brother, my mother, and my niece had just arrived from Houston. The looks on their collective faces depicted the hopelessness we all were experiencing. They struggled to offer a smile, but their expressions of despondency were undeniable.

After exchanging greetings, their first question was, "How is Nic?"

I was not prepared to respond just yet, but somehow, the question took me back to 2003, the year my father died. Back then I had given many family members and friends the news of his death. At some point, everyone had expected to receive the news of my dad's death, since he had battled a long illness and time in hospice care.

Nic's situation was so much different. His death didn't fit the "norm," if there is such a thing. He wasn't doing drugs, he wasn't involved in any criminal activity, and even his car wasn't operational, so he shouldn't have been in a car accident. Hundreds of people die every day from these activities, but no one had any reason to believe he could be included in that number.

Even after receiving the news of a bacterial meningitis attack, everyone still expected a full recovery. We possessed no possibility of thinking any other way. Because of birth order, all parents expect their children to bury them and not the other way around. The certainty of that logic wouldn't allow even the remote possibility of Nic's dying. It was pointless and not worthy of consideration.

Before speaking, I needed a moment or two to organize my words. Hope and desperation filled the looks of my family members and I wanted to give them some sort of encouragement, but, like Falanda, my cup was empty. While surveying the room, my mind and body were not functioning as a cohesive unit. My hands trembled, tears flowed, my thoughts were scrambled, and the emotions of my heart were squashed by death's reality.

Solemnly looking straight at my family, my heart seemed to beat as loud as a bass drum. Nervous, but assured, I uttered the following:

"Nic has been on life support since he was admitted to the hospital and we have reached a point where it's useless to continue. There is absolutely nothing more that can be done and Falanda confirmed what the doctors have been telling us all along. I am so sorry, but my baby is gone. Nic died."

Their stares reminded me of the disbelief of parents when informed by the military their child has been killed in action. The truth of my statement crushed their collective hopes and my family felt the weight of the world fall on their vulnerable shoulders.

After a few minutes of uninterrupted silence, my brother Calvin started crying and his tears turned contagious. Soon, everyone in the room was sobbing. Distraught and anxious, my mother strained to go visit her only grandson. I took her quivering hand and led her along the way. As we walked, my phone blew up with text messages.

The text Falanda had sent reached its intended target, along with its somewhat vague message. It read: "Nico's condition is worsening and we ask that you continue praying for him and for us as we approach this next phase."

Our intent was to delay announcing his death until the next day and also to suggest we had no hope of his recovery. As a result, students overwhelmed the waiting room. So much so, that the hospital recommended we set a time restriction, along with a limit of three to four people at a time. That way, everybody would be accommodated, albeit just a few minutes, to say their goodbyes.

While my family conversed among themselves, Arlene and I made arrangements. We asked Falanda to monitor the visitors' time with Nic after my family concluded theirs. With so many people showing up, we faced another long night and we wanted to assure everyone some time with their much-adored friend.

That very unconventional evening soon passed into a more subdued night filled with love and appreciation. Events from earlier that day had almost created a windstorm of destruction. Ferocious winds ripped away my sanity and faith as if they were an old wooden shack in a barren field. My complete annihilation from my weakened state was a real possibility, had it not been for Nic's friends. The outpouring of their love calmed the disruption I felt by accepting his death.

As the night progressed, students kept pouring into the hospital's waiting room. Arlene, Tiffany, and I took the final opportunity to connect with all the friends he loved so much. The waiting room was packed wall-to-wall with not a dry eye in the room, yet we tried to put on a face of appreciation and encouragement. We did not confirm our decision to stop life support, but we told them he was not getting better and we were suspending all visits beginning the next morning.

Not having to make the same declaration with them as my family, I sensed an underlying suspicion from everyone that their Aggie buddy would not be returning to them. Again, I was near my breaking point when looking into the eyes of all those students. Disbelief and profound sadness was evident on each of their Aggie faces.

While surveying the room, I was overcome with love from them, as if God knew the depths of my pain and had directed their combined compassion to comfort my ailing heart. It felt odd, hurting so deeply and yet, discerning such extravagant love. Their sincerity embraced my soul and somehow their love would sustain me throughout my grieving.

Unquestionably, God was responsible, but why? Why come to my aid now?

Each student took their time to introduce themselves to us. Some hugged us, while others shook our hands, but they all expressed a deep sense of compassion for their friend.

To say I was impressed would be an understatement. Even beyond their strained expressions, I observed with ease their love and concern. They were hurting just as bad as we were and in some strange way, that knowledge eased our pain a little, knowing we were not alone.

The Aggie Spirit was alive and well in that waiting room and I could all but hear Nic say, "See, Dad, this is why I'm an Aggie."

They are one hundred percent connected. When one Aggie falls, they all fall, and when one Aggie triumphs, they all triumph. They were united as one and the bond they shared as fellow Aggies is as legendary as their "Whoop" chant.

The love the students exhibited was exceptional and it warmed my broken heart to know he at last had achieved what he longed for during his brief life. He was accepted all the way by a group of his peers and they respected him for the genuine person God created him to be.

All the demographics that typically separate us—race, religion, politics, socioeconomic status, and sexual orientation—were nonexistent barriers that resulted in a very meaningful and authentic friendship. The miracle we all prayed for didn't occur, but the affection displayed by Nic's friends, the hospital staff, and the entire Aggie family was miraculous in its own right.

It was a long night, one I will never forget.

We decided not to visit with Nic to allow visitors to say their final goodbyes uninterrupted. Before leaving the hospital, we stopped by the nurse's station for one last plea.

By this time, they were well aware of my repeated requests and the nurse answered before I spoke. "We gotcha, Mr. Williams. If there's any change whatsoever, we'll contact you immediately."

With somber hearts and shattered dreams, we all headed to the hotel for our final night's stay.

CHAPTER 7

DAY FOUR

After what seemed like the blink of an eye, crickets outside my window fell silent as morning arrived many hours before expected. My eyes burned from the lack of sleep and my sanity strained from the weight of reality. Knowing the day would include the official death announcement created unlimited thoughts of what if's, why's, and how's. With no answers to the unexplainable, my faith took a nosedive into an abyss.

Listening to various snoring volumes from Arlene and Tiffany, I lay in bed, staring at the circled ceiling patterns made from a painter's brush. My mind played tricks as it reshaped the patterns to resemble a picture of Nic smiling down at me. Throughout the restless night, my hopes of receiving a phone call from the hospital were doomed, but somehow, I still wanted to believe in God's miracle. The phone never rang and the heartbeat of that 'would-be miracle' vanished along with the darkness of the night. Repositioning myself in bed, I turned on my side and stared at the alarm clock.

Tick... tick... tick...

Watching the seconds slowly go by only reminded me that the time was nearing for us to face the excruciating tasks that awaited us. I wanted to smash the damn clock as if it contained powers to suspend time. Impossible, but it was the only alternative remaining that would relieve us from the day's insufferable challenges.

Tick... tick... tick...

"Good morning. It's almost eight and we all need to get up."

Tiffany awoke with a long yawn. "Oooooookay, Dad." With her outstretched arms, she nudged David to wake him up.

Rubbing her eyes, Arlene muttered, "Really? It feels like we just went to bed."

"Yeah, I know. I feel the same way. How was your sleep?" Knowing she slept like a hibernating bear, I inquired anyway.

"I feel so tired. I didn't sleep at all last night."

"Arlene, please! You and Tiffany sounded like chain saws all night. You definitely got a good night's sleep!"

"Dad, was I really snoring, too?"

"Yes, Tootie, for a while I thought you and your mother were in a competition to see who could snore the loudest!"

Tiffany didn't believe me, so I asked David to chime in. "Did you hear them?"

With a broad smile, he said, "No comment, Mr. Williams, I didn't hear a peep."

"Ahhh... Good answer, David. You're outnumbered, but I have your back."

"Um hum." Arlene's voice reeked of sarcasm, but her smile indicated she was well aware of her reputation.

We shared a light moment that we all appreciated and needed. The day would be another difficult one and to start it off with a little humor was a breath of fresh air.

"Let's take our showers, go get breakfast, and then we'll head over to the hospital. Tiffany, you can go first and, remember, there are three of us waiting, so don't take all morning."

I asked Tiffany to go first on purpose to give us an opportunity to speak with David alone. She was still in denial about everything and we wanted to talk with him in private about monitoring her behavior and reporting back to us, should he notice anything out of character. We needed him to keep a close eye on her until she returned home the next week. He agreed and we exchanged phone numbers.

After showering and devouring a breakfast of fruit and cereal, we pulled up to the hospital around 9:30. Upon arrival, we made our ritual beeline to the nurse's station. A different nurse was on duty, but a change in staff didn't dictate a change in Nic's condition. The death sentence diagnosis remained, "No brain activity."

While making his rounds Dr. Cunningham spotted us at the nurse's station and headed our way.

Before he even spoke, I threw my last Hail Mary question. "Is there any experimental treatment or drug that could help Nic?"

Of course, I already knew nothing more could be done, but for the sake of my sanity, all doubt had to be removed.

With a raised eyebrow and biting the left side of his lower lip, Dr. Cunningham could see the desperation in my inquiry. He put his hand on my shoulder. "I wish there was something, Mr. Williams, but there is no experimental treatment or drug for your son's condition. He's brain dead."

That was the first time he used those words. After learning of our appointment with the organ donation people, he had no reason to soften the severity of Nic's condition any longer.

Acceptance of reality now left my heart and soul dead as well.

Tiffany and David went on to the waiting room while Arlene and I prepared to meet with the organ donation people. We asked the nurse to contact the representative and inform them we were ready. Before allowing them to make the call, Arlene gave a very specific directive. "Do not send the same man who approached us Wednesday night."

The nurse complied and informed us the representative would meet with us in ten minutes.

While waiting, Arlene and I exchanged very intuitive looks. We were far from being friends or even cordial before this situation, but at that very moment we connected. Without saying a word, we both wondered, with all that happened, *Was it somehow predestined?*

We remembered the day Nic was born and how Arlene was so worried about his being completely healthy. We remembered the difficulty he had making friends and the real possibility of his committing suicide as a result. We both feared that our past sins had caught up with us and Nic's death was God's retribution.

I wanted to hug her to reassure her that nothing could be further from the truth. Our son's death was just another horrible, but random, event of life.

The ten minutes passed and the organ donation person appeared right on cue. A young woman introduced herself as Mona Sinclair and she ushered us to the nurse's break room. The location was a rather informal location for such a sensitive matter, but we didn't question it and followed her.

She appeared to be in her early 30's and wore a bun hairstyle with dyed red streaks. Her choice to wear a knee-length solid black dress with black high heeled pumps made me wonder if black was her preferred choice, considering the nature of her job. For someone whose job is to discuss the donation of a loved one's organs, she exhibited sincere and heartfelt empathy for her "customers."

Before she began, we told her not to touch Nic

prior to 5:00 p.m. that afternoon. That was the absolute latest they could start the operation to harvest his organs. She gave no debate with our directive.

Although "Acceptance" had secured its position, I was determined to give God every opportunity to perform a miracle, even if it came at the very last second.

She extended her sorrow for our loss and thanked us for our consideration. Her approach was honest and so much more receptive to our concerns compared to the guy they sent earlier. Or, maybe it was our finally accepting Nic's death that made her approach seem more sympathetic.

For such an emotional topic, she described the donation process like a salesman explaining the details of a car loan. She assured us that patients with the greatest need came first. She also mentioned that recipients and the donor's family remain anonymous, but could meet one year later if both parties agree.

Once we got passed the basics, the most critical question emerged. "Do you wish to donate certain organs or all of them?"

It struck me as a rather odd question, but apparently some donor families wish to leave certain organs intact. I didn't understand the logic with that decision, but for me, it really didn't matter.

We agreed to donate all, which included kidneys, lungs, liver, eyes, and his heart. I would never want to meet any recipients of Nic's gifts, regardless of how grateful they were. I would find it too painful looking into his eyes, knowing they no longer held the memories of our time together.

Arlene took the exact opposite approach and didn't have a problem meeting any of them after a year. She wanted to see and feel that in some way our son was still alive.

After going over all the details, a few documents required our signature. Before signing, I had a fleeting moment of reflection.

As a Christian, we believe our bodies are not a means to an end. As a biological being, we have a finite number of days and, at some point, we all will concede to death's calling. We're also taught that, if you accept Jesus as our Lord and Savior, your spirit will live on for eternity in heaven.

Desperately wanting to hold on to that truth, I found myself skeptical, considering all that had occurred. Granted, I had issues with God that didn't necessarily prevent me from believing the young man I love so dearly was eradicated from any and all existence. His spirit had to be alive and one day we would be reunited.

We signed the papers giving the hospital all access. Without question, Nic would have wanted to help others by donating his organs.

Mona thanked us again and offered several publications to assist with our grieving. Hopeful they wouldn't be needed, we took the information and headed back to the waiting room. We made phone calls to our loved ones and informed them that, if there were no change by 5:00 p.m., we would discontinue life support efforts.

They responded with cries of disbelief and some suggested we do this or that, but they all begged us not to give up hope. Of course, they didn't have all the information and we didn't have time or energy to dispute their suggestions. After completing the last call, it was time.

Upon entering the corridor, I found the hustle and bustle of the ICU had slowed to a turtle's pace. The sounds of monitors peeping, televisions game shows, ringing phones, and conversations among nurses all seemed to have transformed into an eerie silence. The large waiting room was completely empty, with no visitors in sight.

The closer we got to Nic's room, the more desolate the walk became. As we made each step, I imagined another step being added, making our destination infinite. The nurse's station was vacated and rooms with windows had their curtains drawn.

Was there a fire drill and everyone heard the alarm but us? Or was it just "Acceptance" clearing an uninhibited path to finality?

During the past 72 hours, so much evidence had pointed to the inevitable truth, but somehow my struggle with the unwarranted reality continued. Everything near and dear to me—my heart, my faith, my hopes, and my dreams—had all been infected by death's claim. My emptied soul was all that remained. Confident we did everything humanly and medically, with absolute faith, to save Nic. However, all our efforts turned out to be in vain.

As we got closer, my breaths labored in the thick air that all of a sudden filled the hospital. My heartbeats slowed to a pace that should have caused me to faint at any second. Imagination or not, my body was now reacting to what my mind had come to terms with. After the visit, I would never see my son alive again.

I wished to produce any reason to delay entry. No more visitors, no more treatments, no miracle, and no more hope. Unanswered prayers and death's claim were now my new normal.

With grief-filled hearts Arlene, Tiffany, and I entered Nic's room to say goodbye to our cherished son and troublesome baby brother. Hurting just as much as they were and being so angry with God, I felt helpless and speechless. Feeling the need to be a pillar of strength for everyone, but I couldn't.

In all honesty, I myself needed someone to lean on.

Looking at his chest inhaling and exhaling air, my eyes were convinced he was alive, but my mind knew the truth. The ventilator kept his lungs breathing enough to sustain his life, and without it, all organs would slowly shut down and his body would die soon afterwards. I opened his eyelid to see if his pupils would respond to the light in the room, but they didn't. I held his hand hoping for any sort of reflective movement, but there was none.

While sitting on the edge of his bed and staring

at his striking facial features, I was convinced God couldn't have created a more handsome young man. As his parents, we would love to take credit for his Leading Man good looks, but they were God-given and not hereditary.

Oooooh, how I wished he could smile just once more and project the warmth and love he genuinely made us all feel.

Knowing his brain was gone and his body would soon follow, I wondered about his soul and his spirit. I hoped they were in the room with us.

Then I led our final good-byes.

"We love you, Nic, with all our hearts and souls! You're the best son any parent anywhere could dream of and you've enriched our lives way beyond our imagination. From the day you were born, it's been an absolute joy watching you grow from a fearless, bowlegged toddler to the charismatic, fun-loving young man you are today. I can't help but think of all the wonderful memories we shared during the past twenty years. Remember when you were about thirteen years old and your voice was just as high-pitched as Tiffany's. Because they sounded exactly the same, people would often confuse the two of you when they called the house. We teased you a lot by comparing your timid little voice to that of a Chihuahua... Yip, yip, yip. I told you when you became a man, you'll have a voice similar to mine, which I proudly characterized as a big dog... Ruff, Ruff, Ruff (with lots of bass). We teased you for years until one day you called me and said, 'Dad, Ruff Ruff' with this very deep baritone sound to your voice. Your vocal maturity had finally arrived and you were so proud of it!! I was proud for you as well even though I had one less thing to tease about you. For the last time, 'Ruff, Ruff, my son'."

I hugged him as his lifeless arms remained at his sides. I smelled him, I caressed his cheeks, I kissed him on his forehead, and again, I told him how much I loved him.

Love was such an inadequate description when expressing the depth of my feelings at that moment. It epitomized an inseparable bond that conquers all and transcends time. Love never reaches a plateau or declines.

Love just is.

I closed my eyes and concentrated with the intensity of penetrating far beyond the realms of his mere body. I focused through the barriers of his physical presence and into his intangibles: his soul, his mind, and his spirit. They are the true essence of his earthly existence and were reclaimed by God at his death. I pushed and pushed passed the limits of my consciousness until convinced we transcended time and space.

We connected. We embraced each other with extreme compassion. We had to say goodbye for now, but I had an assurance, this wasn't the end. My anger towards God was justified, due to my limited human understanding, but after feeling Nic's presence, the spirit of my son would live on and I WILL SEE HIM AGAIN.

Arlene joined in and told a few stories of her most memorable times. For such a heartbreaking occasion, we shared lots of laughter among the anguished sounds associated with a final good-bye.

To my surprise, Tiffany didn't say anything, which only confirmed my suspicion that she was not at the acceptance stage. Her reluctance was a concern, but we didn't insist. We just hoped David took our suggestion to heart.

As the 5:00 deadline neared, Arlene wanted to say one final prayer. I agreed, but refused to lead it. By holding on to my anger, I saw no point in praying to a God who allowed my son to die.

I held Nic's left hand while Arlene held his right hand. We then held Tiffany's hands to form a circle and we bowed our heads to pray. Disappointed, Arlene frowned at me with a bit of sarcastic expression, but she led the prayer.

"Dear God, we come before you with very humble hearts. Our beloved son and brother is in need of your healing grace. The doctors cannot do anything more, but we know all power is within your discretion. We don't want to let him go because we love him and he's a part of us. We aren't perfect, but we have complete faith and trust in you. We accept and believe that you sent your only son Jesus Christ, to die for the sins of the world so we could have everlasting life. If it's your will to call Nic home now, please welcome him into your loving arms and please give us the strength to accept it. Your word says, 'I can do everything through him who gives me strength.' We ask that you honor your word and give us the strength to get through the very difficult days that await us. We ask this in Jesus name, Amen."

After the prayer, we said our goodbyes and 'I love you' one final time. By instinct, I wanted to stay by his side until the very last second before being wheeled away, but my grief prevented it. My last sight had to be of him "sleeping" and not being wheeled away to have his body cut up for its organs.

We exited the room and blew him a kiss. "Goodbye for now, my son."

As we passed the nurse's station, they stopped us to give us Nic's belongings. I glanced in the bag, not expecting to see anything other than his clothes. Upon close inspection, I stopped dead in my tracks and wanted to burst out laughing, but it just wasn't in me.

Like most parents, Arlene never failed to tell the monsters, "Always wear decent underwear. You never know when you may be in an accident or something that would require them to be removed."

Here was proof Nic didn't get that message, because his boxers had a couple of holes in them. Smiling with tears in my eyes, I visualized his embarrassment.

Searching a little further, I found his wallet. As usual, he didn't have a dollar to his name. Smiling once again, it reminded me of all his calls asking for a loan. Like the boxers, laughter was my immediate response, but the urge quickly vanished. Seeing his driver's license, student ID, bank card, medical ID, and social security card, it hit me that those are the identity documents that represent a person's life and he no longer needed them. I closed the wallet.

The question of WHY kept re-entering my mind and I found it increasingly more difficult to block it out.

Out of the blue, a saying I heard many years ago popped into my head. "When a spouse dies, the surviving spouse is called a widower. When young parents die, their children are called orphans. So, what's the term attributed to parents when their child dies? There isn't one because a child's death should never occur before their parent's."

We took Nic's identity documents and headed towards the exit doors of his life. The hospital staff and everything around us seemed to have transformed back to its normalcy. The nurses were back at their station, sounds from the patient's televisions had resumed, and visitors now walked up and down the corridors.

Our goodbyes were complete.

CHAPTER 8

THE CHOICE

While packing and preparing to leave College Station, I remembered an earlier phone call from my good friend, Sarah Hinojosa. She had done a little research and suggested something that didn't really resonate with me at first. Trying to digest Nic's death and planning a funeral occupied every available brain cell and left me no room to focus on anything else.

But, as the day wore on, Sarah's phone call ignited a passion and purpose that could ensure Nic's death wasn't in vain. Nothing could ever replace my loss, but knowing something good could come from his death was an opportunity worth exploring.

Texas law requires college students who live in dorms to be vaccinated for bacterial meningitis. Sarah asked if Nic lived in a dorm. Because A&M's dorms were all filled when he was a freshman, he lived in an off campus apartment. She then asked why the law only applied to students living in a dorm.

Agreed, it didn't make much sense, but again

my mind was a million miles away. She suggested, when time permits, I should look into it and maybe do something about it. Without realizing it, Sarah planted a seed that grew far beyond anything I ever imagined.

While pacing in the hotel lobby and thinking about that conversation, the proverbial light bulb illuminated in my head. If that law had included all students, Nic would have been required to be vaccinated and quite possibly he would be alive and well.

Contemplating that concept, I felt compelled to make a few inquiries. But to do so required an association with a state politician or an attorney with political connections. To my dismay, I didn't know any of either profession. Then, Stud's name appeared like a flashing billboard sign!

My very best friend, Dwight "Stud" Boykins, was just the person who could hook me up with any local politician or lawyer. We've been best friends for decades and were each other's best man in our respective weddings. Stud is about 6'2", denies he has a potbelly, and has the ability to convince a blind man to buy a set of binoculars. God blessed him with the "gift of gab" and he used it to propel himself in the cutthroat world of political lobbying.

We both have the same nickname, "Stud." He refers to me as Stud # 2, as I do him. Unable to recall the details of why we refer to ourselves as studs, but I'm sure it had something to do with our past romances. Viewing Stud as my little brother, and watching him grow from an insecure young man to a successful businessman and a Houston city councilman was an astonishing achievement. He maintained lots of political contacts and friends in high places, so I was more than confident he could assist me.

He suggested a Texas state legislator from the Sugar Land area. It needed to be someone who could explain why the law only applied to students living in a dorm and possibly assist me with changing it to include all students. I had no idea of the journey on which I was about to embark.

Stud didn't let me down. He contacted Rep. Charlie Howard, the long-term state representative from Sugar Land, and he spoke with him about my situation. He assured me that Rep. Howard would call soon.

"Hello, Mr. Williams, this is Rep. Charlie Howard, state representative from Sugar Land. I hope you don't mind me calling at such a difficult time for you and your family."

"Hello, Rep. Howard. I don't mind at all. I was the one who initiated the call and I appreciate you finding the time."

"A Mr. Dwight Boykins contacted my office and asked that I give you a call. I understand your family is a member of the district I serve and I would like to help anyway I can."

"I assume Dwight brought you up to speed regarding my son's situation?"

"Yes, he did."

"It hasn't been released to the media yet, but we discontinued life support efforts and my son's death will be announced shortly."

"Oh, Mr. Williams, I'm sorry to hear that news. We all have been following his story and praying for his recovery."

"Thank you, sir. This is so unexpected. I just hope we can survive it."

"If you don't mind, I would like to share with you my own personal story. It may help you and your family during this most difficult time."

"Sure, please go right ahead."

Knowing the hospital was about to harvest Nic's organs made me want to cry out in agony. By dealing with my own personal tragedy, my mind didn't have the capacity to consider someone else's. By good fortune, my senses returned and I realized Rep. Howard was attempting to console me and offer words of encouragement.

"Greg, I, too, lost a son. It's something you never get over, but with God's grace and mercy we were able to maintain our faith and accept his untimely death as part of God's plan. It happened many, many years ago, but it still feels like yesterday. Our son was a little boy when he drowned in the lake behind our house. My wife thought he was with me and I thought he was with her. Our hearts were panic-filled with the horrible thought he may have wandered off and drowned in the lake. At the same time, our hearts were filled with the hope that he wasn't anywhere near the lake. Unfortunately, that's exactly where he wondered off. We're a Christian family and our faith is the only thing that got us through those terrible days. If you don't mind, may I ask if you believe in God?"

"Don't mind at all and, yes, we are Christians."

"I'm so glad to hear that. You will be tested beyond your belief, but never forget God is with you every step of the way. Keep your eyes focused on him, and you and your family will make it through these dark days. I'll be praying for you."

Everything Rep. Howard said was meant to encourage me and to help maintain my faith in God, but that was not the conversation I sought. Maybe later, but not at that moment. I needed to know what the legislature could do to prevent what happened to Nic from ever happening to another unsuspecting college student.

I continued, "We will, Rep. Howard, and we do appreciate your prayers. We'll be leaving College Station in an hour or so after the announcement becomes official, but there is one subject I would like to discuss with you, if you have a few more minutes."

"Sure, anything."

"Does Texas have a law that requires college students who live in a dorm to be vaccinated against meningitis? If so, why does the law only apply to students who live in a dorm? And lastly, what can be done to modify the law and require all students to be vaccinated? Before leaving College Station this evening, I wanted to speak with someone who could track down those answers for me. Can you help me?"

"Consider it done. I can tell you now that during the last legislative session, a meningitis law was passed, but I'm not aware of the details at this moment. I'll look into it and we'll talk in a day or so. Don't worry about this. Go home and take care of your family."

"Will do, sir, and thank you for your time."

The 5:00 deadline arrived with no phone call from the hospital. Although I had no reason to believe there would be, still, my hope remained intact. Pacing up and down the hotel's lobby while searching the face of the wall clock every few seconds, I felt my self-inflicted agony nearing its end.

Arlene watched me the whole time and she sensed my pain of wishful expectation. She knew to let me arrive at the "it's over" destination without disturbing me. I had to come to terms with it in my own time.

At about 5:30, I did. My mind softly blew out the candle of hope in my heart and I conceded the final time.

God failed us at our most desperate hour.

☆ ☆ ☆

ONCE THE CARS WERE PACKED, it came time for us to leave College Station. We hugged Tiffany for what seemed like an hour and we still didn't want to let her go. When you lose a child, you by nature become overprotective of any remaining children, but our reasoning for the extended embrace went beyond. This hug was our last opportunity to connect our emotions to what we all just experienced. It was an embrace of memories, love, support, and strength to help us get through the unrelenting pain.

We had no reason to stay any longer, yet abandoning my child was a feeling that still haunted me. In my mind's eye, a young Nic cried out to me for help, but I couldn't get to him. As much as I tried and tried, something pulled him farther and farther away until his cries grew silent in the distance.

I failed him.

Opening the car door, I remembered when we first arrived, with the expectation of Nic returning home with us a foregone conclusion. Never in my wildest imagination would we leave without him unless he fully recovered and decided to stay at his beloved Aggie Land. If the whole ordeal were repeated a thousand times over and, even with my knowing the outcome, still, I never believed he would die. Never!

We started the hour-and-a-half trip home, while Tiffany and David headed back to San Antonio. About thirty minutes after leaving the hotel, my phone rang and the unexpected noise made me jump. It was the hospital and my anxiety skyrocketed to the heavens!!

My heart was racing with the anticipation a miracle had indeed arrived albeit at the very last second!!! My gleeful eyes met Arlene's blank stare. Certainly, she had to be thinking the same thing. Not wanting to get her hopes up, she kept her emotions in check.

Could it be? Could it really be the miracle we'd prayed so hard?

Pulling over and parking the car was a must, due to the unpredictability of my reactions, should the call be what we hoped. Taking several deep breaths had no effect on my pending celebration! It was a full hour after the deadline and the only possible reason to call would be a change in Nic's condition.

We had no time to pray, but an ole biblical theory came to my mind, a saying among the elderly: "God may not be there when you want him, but he's always on time."

That wisdom had to be true for us, and it would become my life's testimony. I answered the phone with the urgency of an unfolding miracle, "Hello, this is Greg Williams."

"Hello, Mr. Williams, this is Mona from the hospital and I'm calling to inform you that Nicolis is going into surgery now."

"Surgery... Really??" It took everything in me not to scream an obscenity at Mona.

Why on earth would she call to tell me that?

It's not like he's going into surgery with the possibility of having his health restored. Yes, he was having surgery, but it wouldn't benefit him, so why call me? It made more sense to call the appointed recipients with the news, rather than the donor's family.

While Mona's intent was no doubt meant to keep me informed, I found it torturous instead. The depth of my disappointment prevented me from responding and with an abrupt click I ended the call.

Finally over, we had no miracle to claim or celebrate. If I possessed the power, my favorite bible verse would read:

Trust in the LORD with all your heart; and lean not on your own understanding. In all your ways acknowledge him and he "MAY" make your paths straight.

Proverbs 3:5-6

Arlene's face shot me a look of 'I told you so,' but she dared not say it.

Full of anger and frustration, I pounded the steering wheel, trying to get God's attention. After a few minutes of cooling off, I started the car and headed down the desolate highway of despair.

During the drive, we often asked each other, "Are you okay?" And we both responded with a convenient lie, "Yes." We should have talked more, but the pain was too deep.

The drive back was the exact opposite compared to our initial drive to A&M. This time my anger prevented me from talking. At first, I had so much faith and confidence in God that the possibility of Nic's death was as distant as the farthest galaxies. After praying with such confidence and believing in God's mercy, how could he fail us?

Now, the truth of the matter was, *Nic was dead and God was to blame.*

With over 48,000 students enrolled at Texas A&M, why was Nic stricken with a meningitis attack and why did it have to be to death's extent? When horrible things happen, Christians by nature turn to God for answers, and many times if feels as though our inquiries fall on deaf ears. Plenty of questions regarding God's motives can create serious doubt, even among the most devout believer, but this is the very time when one needs to have resolute faith. Faith is developed by experiencing God's love and then reinforced after subsequent experiences that require hope and trust in God.

So, what happens when you have an experience where the result isn't a positive reinforcement to one's faith?

You continue to praise God in all situations and believe that, although things may not go the way you desire, trust him and know he loves you.

Rejoice always, pray continually, give thanks in all circumstances; for this is God's will for you in Christ Jesus.

1 Thessalonians 5:16-18)

That scripture was the farthest one from my mind and one I couldn't accept when Nic's life was at stake. Prayer and faith were my only comfort in believing my son would be healed and when he died, "giving thanks" was impossible.

Nic's ordeal was the only time in my entire life when I prayed and believed with all sincerity and commitment, yet God deserted me. Anger and disbelief replaced prayer and faith and at that point, a critical choice had to be made.

I needed God, but how could I believe in him after he failed my son?

My mind searched for comfort scriptures, but my anger led to dead ends. In spite of my rage, to survive the "next steps," I needed peace, which only God could provide. Without it, I wanted to be shut off from the world and deal with my loss in my own private way. And, without it, I couldn't take the initiative and do the activities that required my immediate attention.

The death of one's child doesn't follow the sequential order of life as we expect it and as a result, part of you dies along with them. What remains is an emotional emptiness that can never be filled. That emptiness raised very valid questions regarding my faith, but I still could not deny what was deep within my soul, that God is real and he loves me!

Trying to understand "why" was a futile exercise and a complete waste of time. To get through whatever lay ahead, the "Why" question had to be put to rest. Holding on to the belief that God loves me unconditionally and allowing him to guide me through the minefield of agony and confusion was my only hope for peace of mind. I was unsure that was even possible, knowing my anger and disappointment conquered all rational thoughts.

But I chose God anyway.

CHAPTER 9
RECONCILIATION

Seeing my own bed was a welcoming sight, and experiencing the layers of its comfort was far more soothing than anything a stiff drink could offer. Both were a necessity, but passing up the drink and jumping straight into bed provided immediate relief. With all the restless nights and sleeping in an overcrowded hotel room, my bed represented an oasis of rest. The softness of the silky satin sheets and feeling the memory foam mattress contour to the shape of my body was truly hypnotic. I was out in seconds.

The next morning we met at Arlene's church to plan the arrangements. Windsor Village United Methodist is a mega church with thousands of members. With such a large congregation, ample ministries are available for the benefit of its parishioners. The Comfort and Care Ministry provides guidance to families in need of assistance with funeral arrangements.

Although the process was hardly routine for us,

we accomplished a lot because of the established procedures. So many activities were predetermined, which made the decision-making process so much easier. The service couldn't last any longer than an hour, which meant the number of speakers and length of time for each was very limited. Add in the eulogy, a few songs, and we could call it a wrap.

The most emotional task was selecting a program to describe Nic's brief life. While viewing so many types of programs, I couldn't help but notice the faces of all the deceased. Young, old, children, men, women, veterans, mothers, fathers… and the list goes on and on. A once vibrant life, now reduced to a few color or black and white pages, depending on affordability.

So many deaths, so much heartache to develop those programs, yet they were presented like vacation brochures to choose among. Try this one… Or, how about that one…

I wondered if Nic's program would be presented in the same manner. *Would someone question his story?*

Probably not. Without the emotion, death is just another business, a milestone in life, which we all will patronize at some point.

We left the meeting with the assignment of writing an obituary and submitting pictures of Nic's life.

The following day, we drove back to A&M for the difficult task of cleaning out Nic's room and returning home with all his belongings. Passing through the working-class neighborhood, I noticed the modest homes featured well-established pine trees and sparsely developed landscaping. The sun pierced through the thick shaded leaves as we approached the house, a rental property, for the first time.

With pine needles almost ankle high and overgrown grass, the residence didn't look the norm. As we exited the car, my thoughts wandered back to Nic's freshman year. The law requiring freshman to be vaccinated was not implemented until 2009, but he had started college in the fall of 2008. His fate was sealed.

His three roommates greeted us with solemn looks and offered to help us in any way they could. Just days earlier we met them for the first time in the midst of so much hope and anticipation. None of us thought the result would lead to despair and death.

We wanted the opportunity to sit and talk with the young men at length, but a very tight schedule prevented us. Nic was right. They seemed to be very nice young men from good families. He had no issues with them, despite their being fans of Glen Beck.

I was always amazed at Nic's ability to blow things off. During his life, he never saw appalling behavior in anyone. Everybody got a pass. He truly loved people and all he ever wanted was their acceptance.

Once during his senior year in high school, a small group of friends met him at work just before he was scheduled to get off. Kids being kids, they played around in Panera Bread's parking lot and decided to write a message on the back windshield of his car.

They wrote "Nic is cool for a black guy."

He drove home with that insulting message while his friends followed close behind. We were furious with him for allowing them to do it and even more so for driving home and broadcasting it.

Our disappointment was also directed towards his so-called "friends." If they were indeed his true friends, could they not see how offensive their message was to Nic? They had apologized, but he hadn't taken it as seriously and dismissed it as a silly prank.

After leading us to Nic's bedroom, the boys left us to ourselves, but were available if we needed them. The room was his home-away-from-home, and I couldn't help but feel we were violating his space. He would never enter that room again nor sleep in his own bed at home.

His privacy should not have been an issue, but not everything died the moment he did. Somehow that day reminded me of the day I helped him move in his freshman year, one of the best days of our lives. We both expected to re-live that excitement after graduation and he moved out.

But plans change and now I experienced no excitement... only tears.

A bit of shock was our first impression. Nic's room was spotless. Everything was properly positioned as if it was just cleaned by room service. All the years of constant demands to pick up his clothes and clean his room must have taken root. What a nice surprise! But minutes later, a discovery led us to believe otherwise. When we opened his closet door, clothes and junk came pouring out and almost knocked us both over.

Now, that was the Nic we knew and loved.

Several comical posters adorned his wall, which reflected his crazy sense of humor. He was a proud member of FLIP (Freshman Leaders in Progress) and we found many trinkets that had reminded him and anyone who entered his room of his membership. Neon green was their group color. Picture frames, hats, painted rocks, sunglasses, clothes—everything he owned—all were that loud shade of green!

After walking around trying to imagine how he spent time in his room, I sat on his bed and closed my eyes. Smelling his scent, I imagined him walking through the door with his wide grin and calling me "Dad."

By the simple way he enunciated the word, I could always determine what he wanted. A quick and sudden "Dad" meant he was stressed about something and he needed advice. A slow and drawn out "Daaad" more than likely indicated he needed money or some sort of favor. If he raised his voice, he was very excited about something and he couldn't wait to share the news.

The "Dad" I will miss the most is the "Declaration Dad." He ended every conversation by saying "Dad," a slight pause, and then he followed up with, "You know I love you?"

The thought called to mind my own dad and all

the years we missed out by not hearing those three simple words that mean soooo much. As a parent, nothing is more comforting than knowing your child loves you and appreciates your efforts and the sacrifices you made for them.

Hearing and interpreting Nic's "Dad" is gone forever, but I'm so thankful for the times I did.

Smiling, I opened my eyes to a view of his nightstand and discovered an envelope turned upside down. After flipping it over, I recognized my handwriting, but not the name written on it. "Nico" instead of Nic. It was the same letter I had given to him a couple of months earlier, but I don't recall writing "Nico." We always called him Nic, so why did I write Nico?

I gasped in disbelief, leaned against the headboard, and searched my thoughts. The envelope, dated November 11th, exactly three months prior to the date he died, was opened, so he had read the letter at some point.

Memories of people and conversations came flooding, creating a flashback of scenes to a complicated movie plot. The images were constant and repetitive. The letter, the urgency with writing it, Sarah telling me about her feelings that her son Nico would die at an early age, Trish telling me about God's plan for my life and *The Shack*, all inundated my confused state like a gigantic jigsaw puzzle, but the pieces wouldn't connect.

My head spun from the mosaic of thoughts and

images, along with all the conflicting interpretations they represented. Only minutes passed, but it seemed like an eternity before things started to blend into one central idea. Not sure if my desperate need to rationalize Nic's death or a higher power directed my thoughts, I wondered if something out of the ordinary was the impetus behind the idea.

Of course, the higher power had to be God, but my choosing to remain committed to my faith wasn't one hundred percent just yet and some residual doubt lingered. As my concentration intensified, the message became crystal clear. The images, signs, and messages were all premonitions of Nic's death.

Could Sarah's message of her son's premature death have been intended for my son who now went by the name of Nico? Because Nico was never accepted as Nic's nickname, Sarah's conviction failed to register with me. But, the moment I turned the envelope over, I knew in an instant the death she predicted was meant for my son "Nico," and not hers by the same name.

The purpose in writing my letter had provided an opportunity to say goodbye without the knowledge of Nic's pending death. Although the intent of the letter was a different matter, my "I Love You" message was unmistakable. We wouldn't be together at the time of his death, but I took comfort in knowing he realized how much I loved him.

Of the three premonitions, Trish's prediction of God's plan for my life was the most revealing. Even though the grief and hurt would prove unbearable, I couldn't permit the "Great Sadness" or depression to overtake me the way it did with the character, Mack. The story reminded me of a friend who lost his son about three years earlier. The doctors were helpless in treating his son's respiratory ailment and he died within a couple of days. The friend had been a very devoted and faithful Christian, but he lost it after the death of his son. He was so angry with God that he never attended church again.

The recollection of that particular memory at that exact time and place was no coincidence.

The letter, Sarah's conviction, and Trish's message all pointed to Nic's premature death. I had no way to interpret it at the time and maybe it was best I didn't. The revelation created a rising tidal wave of awareness and purpose deep within my spirit. Now with a job to do, I couldn't allow my grieving prevent me from the possibility of saving the lives of others who otherwise would be susceptible to the same fate as Nic.

The current meningitis law at the time of Nic's death—The Jamie Schanbaum Act—required students living in a dorm to be vaccinated, but what about the students who didn't? Don't they congregate and interact with those who live in a dorm? Why protect one segment of the student body and not all of them?

My logic suggested if the law included all students, maybe Nic's death could have been prevented.

At that point, I understood what Trish meant about God having a plan for my life. Some wise soul said there are two great days in our lives, the day we are born and the day we discover why we're born.

That day was my "why" moment.

We hurried to pack all of Nic's clothes, his bed, his computer, and everything that was reflective of who he had been, who he was currently, and who he was becoming. After loading everything in the U-Haul trailer, we stopped to thank the roommates for all they had done and for befriending Nic. We told them how much he respected them and how much fun he had being around them.

More words might have flowed from both sides, but silence prevailed. An unexpected death has a strange way of stealing moments of reflection and expression. The embrace we shared with them said it all.

On the trip back to Houston, I didn't share any of my thoughts with Arlene for fear of criticism. I needed additional time to solidify and defend my position.

Was my revelation far-fetched in reaching the conclusions I claimed? What happened to my loss of faith and my anger towards God? Was I in a subconscious way diverting my grief and channeling my energies into something more constructive?

My doubts were obvious, but I made a decision. I was committed to doing everything within my power to ensure Nic's tragedy would never happen again.

Questioning why Nic's life wasn't spared will never be answered; however, after accepting the revelation, I entertained no doubt my faith would be restored to accomplish the purpose God placed in my heart.

For the first time since the beginning of the whole ordeal, a higher calling led me. How to respond—instead of asking why—was God's response to my search for an explanation. Nic was gone and no one could do anything to change that outcome. However, my new purpose provided me a sense of renewal and determination that solidified the fact that his death would not be in vain!

I could almost feel my faith returning and replenishing my soul with a purpose that wouldn't be denied.

After arriving at Arlene's home and unpacking Nic's things, she asked me to stay a while. Several friends would be coming by to express their condolences and she also agreed to an interview with a local television station. Talking about Nic was easy, but acknowledging his death would take its toll on us both.

Nic's godparents, Floyd and Deborah, stopped by, along with other neighbors, family members, and close friends. While waiting for the television crew to arrive, Floyd received a phone call from his and Arlene's pastor, Kirbyjon Caldwell.

Pastor Caldwell is the dynamic leader of Windsor Village United Methodist Church. Aside from his pastoral responsibilities, he's a very astute businessman and politically well-connected. Floyd is a very close confidant to Pastor Caldwell and volunteers as a prayer minister for the church.

After chatting with Floyd for a moment, Pastor Caldwell asked to speak with me. I took the phone and spoke with the very captivating and devout man of God. At first, he wanted to know how we were holding up. After several minutes of discussing our status, we talked about what happened to Nic and our plans of assuring something like this would never happen again. I explained we were working with a state representative to possibly change the current law.

Pastor Caldwell can be very direct, so I wasn't surprised when he said, "Who's working on this with you?"

"Rep. Charlie Howard from Sugar Land."

"What is he doing specifically?"

"He's working on some legislation to change the current law."

He suggested I ask Rep. Howard to speak at Nic's funeral. I had no idea at the time, but his intent was to encourage Rep. Howard to commit in public that he would do everything within his legislative authority to get the law modified. Rep. Howard had already appeared on television speaking about Nic's unfortunate death and how it should have been prevented.

Rep. Howard was a sincere man, a believer, and he would be committed to do whatever he could to change the law. Later, when I called to extend an invitation to speak at the funeral, he accepted without hesitation.

Floyd also informed us that Pastor Caldwell would perform Nic's service. Now that came as a total shock, because he typically doesn't do funerals unless it's someone really significant or a long-term member of the church. With such a large congregation, the associate pastors are assigned those responsibilities, so we never even considered asking him.

Maybe the change could have been attributed to Pastor Caldwell's relationship with Floyd, but whatever "it" was, something was definitely "in the air."

As the evening progressed, the house was filled with people stopping by to offer their condolences. I accepted each guest's words of sorrow and encouragement, but at the same time detested the purpose of their visit. With so much noise and conversations, I couldn't hear a phone ring.

Mine was set on vibrate when the caller ID read "unlisted." I didn't answer it, so they called right back and that time I clicked the green button.

"Hello, is this Mr. Greg Williams?"

"Yes, it is."

"Mr. Williams, this is Dodie Osteen of Lakewood Church."

I almost dropped the phone. *Why on earth would she be calling me?* I didn't know what to call her, the very popular, Ms. Dodie or Ms. Osteen. I settled for the more respectful, Ms. Osteen.

"Hello, Ms. Osteen. Excuse me if I sound surprised."

"Oh, please don't be. Did I catch you at a bad time?"

Still numb, I said, "No, not at all."

"Our staff was contacted today and we were informed that you're a member of Lakewood Church."

With pride swelling, I said, "Yes, I sure am."

"Greg, I've been following your son's story in the news and I'm so sorry to hear that he went to heaven. How are you and your family doing?"

"It's been really, really tough, but we're managing okay for now."

In all sincerity, she said, "Well, please know that your Lakewood family are all praying for you and your family."

"That's very comforting and we appreciate all the prayers."

"Greg, have the arrangements been made? Would you like to have the service at Lakewood or have you made other plans?"

"Oh, thank you so much for the offer, but, yes, the service is scheduled at Windsor Village United Methodist Church. That's my son's church home, so the service will be held there."

"I know Kirbyjon well. Pastor Caldwell is one of my best friends. Please let us know if we can help in any way."

"Ms. Osteen, I do have one question. How did you know to contact me?"

"Your friend, Linda Kellough, called and informed our staff that you were a member of Lakewood. Was that okay?"

"Sure, I'm glad she did."

"So am I. Be blessed and I'll see you at Lakewood."

"Thank you for calling, Good night, Ms. Osteen."

I had Linda to thank for that phone call and it was not a surprise when Ms. Dodie mentioned her name. Outside of Stud, Linda's my very best friend.

God had sent two angels to help me through my storm.

After the conversation ended, incredible was the only word to describe what had just occurred. The world-renowned Dodie Osteen called and extended an invitation to hold Nic's service at the largest church in America. Hers was not a routine gesture. Something extraordinary was developing in much the same way when Pastor Caldwell had volunteered to do the services. People go to Dodie Osteen and not the other way around, so I was wonderfully blessed that she took time to call me herself.

After telling Arlene about the conversation, she wanted to confirm the services were already scheduled. Of course they were and, regardless of my excitement, no way would a change be made. Dodie Osteen and Kirbyjon Caldwell. *Wow, it just doesn't get any bigger than that!!*

After thanking everyone for their love and support, I headed home to write Nic's obituary.

CHAPTER 10

HOME GOING

In the African American community, the term "Funeral" or "Services" are seldom used to describe a program for the death of a love one. "Home Going" is the preferred expression, appropriate and justifiable for people of faith. For many, the thought of "going home" is a place of tranquility, happiness, and unconditional love.

What better way to describe the destination of eternity?

"Going home" implies affectionate images of loving relationships and peace of mind, amid an environment absent of pain. While the terms "Funeral" and "Home Going" both represent death, the latter is more palatable, because death isn't the end. Believers view it as merely a transition from the world we know to one of heaven's bliss.

As a small child, I wish my family had explained death to me as "going home" instead of as the end of life. At about six years old, I was scarred forever while attending a funeral where I witnessed a relative escorted out of the church during her hysterical outburst after viewing her deceased love one.

It should be illegal to display the remains of the deceased. Yes, people want to see the departed one last time, but what do they really see? The "Remains" are just the physical leftovers and don't represent whom the person was or the life they lived, only the body they just so happened to be born with.

What good is a body without the personality, the character, and the essence of the soul that once occupied it? If funerals are now considered a celebration of life, why exhibit a body that only accentuates death? Programs often exhibit pictures of the deceased person's life, which include family, smiles, and good times. That should be sufficient and celebrated rather than displaying their lifeless "Remains."

Taking two over-the-counter sleeping pills the night before the funeral had no effect on me. The barrage of thoughts associated with attending my child's funeral proved too much for the chemically induced sleep I so needed. The nightmare that had started eleven days earlier would finally conclude at 2:00 p.m., but the heartbreak would remain with me until my last breath.

Lying in bed the morning of the service, I wished my imagination could by magic fast-forward me past the service to Arlene's house where everyone gathered afterwards. Or a clone could pose as my double, allowing me to escape the agony of attending. I even wished for a sudden medical emergency that required immediate hospitalization.

Either scenario was preferable than saying goodbye to yesterday and to tomorrow.

The thought of attending created an uncontrollable flood of heartache which no levy, reservoir, or dam could contain. But, as the restoration of my faith continued, the rushing waters slowed to a trickle. To make it through the day, prayer would be my only refuge.

Pulling back the comforter of my bed, I reached for my old beat-up bible on the nightstand and searched for an appropriate scripture. Upon finding one, I got out of bed and knelt down to pray:

"Father, I kneel before you in need of comfort and peace of mind. My heart is broken and my mind is troubled at the very thought of attending Nic's funeral today. You are a God of peace and your word says,

Peace I leave with you; my peace I give you. I do not give to you as the world gives. Do not let your hearts be troubled and do not be afraid.
John 14:27

"Lord, I ask that you comfort me, Arlene, and Tiffany and give us peace as we say goodbye to Nic today. I ask this of you in Jesus' name. Amen."

☆ ☆ ☆

THE VIEWING BEGAN AT noon and the service followed at 1:00 p.m., so I had a few hours to kill before arriving at Arlene's. Throughout the morning, reflections of Nic's life persisted, like flipping pages of an old picture album. All are cherished memories and never to be forgotten, but one in particular stood out.

While attending A&M, Nic had gone on a camping trip, but called me about 2:00 AM. When any parent receives a call at that time of night, you perceive something is wrong and I am no exception.

Everything was fine, but Nic wanted to call and tell me he loved me. His friends were having a big discussion around the campfire about how mean or absent their fathers were in their lives. He informed them the descriptions of their fathers were so foreign to him because his dad was always supportive and he could depend on no one more than me. He said I was the best father ever and told them, "I love my dad."

Realizing he had a few beers, I asked if he was okay and he was. At that time of morning, his safety was more of a concern, so his confession of love for me hadn't yet sunk in.

But now, the memory of that conversation assured me of my commitment from all those years ago. Saying goodbye would still be painful, but having no regrets ensured me peace of mind.

After reminiscing a couple of hours, I got dressed in my Johnny Cash attire and headed towards Arlene's. I appreciated a peaceful 45-minute drive until I turned the corner. The sight of the limo and police escort, along with the neighbors gawking like spectators at some sort of neighborhood incident, assaulted my peace. Their presence was a gesture of support, but I preferred our privacy.

In my mind, I screamed, *What the Hell Do You Expect to See!!!* but instead, I opted for polite manners and waved while exiting the car.

Once I entered the house, Arlene greeted me. "Good morning, Greg."

"Morning, how you holding up?"

"Tired, I was up all night."

"Well, that makes two of us, but I guess that's to be expected. It's not every day you attend your own child's funeral."

Her eyes were bloodshot, but I had no way to tell if it was due to crying or a lack of sleep. I asked again about her condition. "Are you going to be okay?"

"I'm doing the best I can. I just want to get through this day."

"With God's grace, we'll be fine."

"How's Tootie?"

"She seems okay for the moment. She, David, and a couple friends from college are in her bedroom."

"Good for her. She needs all the support she can get right now. You know, David hasn't called me at all and that concerns me. Has he called you?"

"No, Greg, he hasn't. And I'm concerned too, but I guess we have to trust him."

"Yup, he's all we got in San Antonio, unless she wants to come home for a semester."

Eyebrows raised at my suggestion, Arlene said, "This is her last semester and no way would she take a break."

"It was just a suggestion. In her state of mind right now, I'm not sure she can concentrate on her studies."

"Well, let's talk with her about it later."

"Cool. It's around 11:20 and we need to leave in a few."

☆ ☆ ☆

AT EXACTLY 11:30, WE pulled away in the limo and headed to Nic's life celebration or a destination of despair. To my displeasure, a few gawkers remained outside until we turned the corner. Tiffany and her three girlfriends chatted in small talk while Arlene and I sat in silence still pondering how and why.

Earlier, I'd given the funeral director strict instructions to close the casket before we arrived. We didn't want Tiffany to see her brother in a casket and have that image haunt her the rest of her life. I wanted to protect her from what I experienced only days earlier. We were required to confirm Nic's appearance at the mortuary in preparation for the service and I dreaded the trip. No amount of counseling, no level of support, or anything humanly possible can prepare a parent to view the lifeless body of their child. Even with an abundance of strength derived from unwavering faith and prayer, the task is unbearable at best and leaves a visual scar that will never heal or be forgotten.

I texted again to inform the director we were en route and he would receive another text when we reached the church's parking lot. At that point, the casket was to be closed, regardless of what anybody says.

He texted back, "Got it." He also told me the church was packed to capacity.

Not knowing how many to expect, we hoped all his friends would pay their last respects and it seemed they did.

I whispered to Arlene, "The church is full."

Through a forced smile she said, "That's good. I'm sure Nic is up there smiling and thinking, really, all of this for me."

I couldn't have agreed more.

As expected, the remainder of the trip was quiet and solemn. Staring out the tinted windows, I watched cars yield, giving us the right-of-way as a sign of respect. When witnessing a funeral procession, most people look out of curiosity and then chalk it up as a part of life. As life progresses, we all will make that unavoidable journey, but we are foolish to believe it won't be anytime too soon. We assume we'll be a ripe old age when the grim reaper pays us that unwanted visit, but that assumption is just that, an assumption.

In reality, death can arrive at any time, at any place, and for anyone. Of course it's inescapable, but when it occurs with a young person, we're reminded how precious life is and how it should never be taken for granted.

As I turned around to glance at Arlene and Tiffany, I interpreted their expressions to suggest anywhere else in the world was better than riding in that limo.

We pulled into the parking lot and I sent my final text, "Close it."

Almost fifty family members gathered outside the church, waiting for our arrival. Pastor Caldwell, Stud, and several others lingered as well.

From the corner of my eye I caught a TV station's van parked on the street. *Why?*

The limo driver opened my door and one by one we exited the limo like celebrities, but pallbearers awaited us instead of the paparazzi.

As we approached the church's entrance, a pair of sunglasses to conceal my teary eyes would've been a godsend or, even better, a mask to project an image that all was good. It wasn't. Once we got closer to the entrance, people parted, allowing us to make our way to the front.

Standing next to Pastor Caldwell and approaching me at a quick pace was the matriarch of the Osteen family herself, Dodie Osteen! Speechless, I stuttered again because of her surprise appearance. She eased my awkwardness by introducing herself and informing me to just call her what everyone else does, simply, Ms. Dodie.

"Ms. Dodie, I had no idea you were coming. You didn't mention it when we spoke the other night."

"I know, but I followed your son's story and I could tell he was a godly young man. Even though I never met him, there was something very special about him. And, when I discovered you are a member of Lakewood, I wanted to see if you would like to hold his service there or where it was going to be held."

"Thank you so much for those kind words. He was indeed a very special young man and I will miss him dearly. Had I known you were attending, I would have scheduled you as one of the speakers."

"Oh, don't be concerned. I just came to be with the family, but I spoke to Kirbyjon and he has already given me a minute or two."

"Oh, that's great!"

"Greg, do you ever go to Wednesday night service at Lakewood?"

"Yes, every week."

"Good. I want to invite you to sit with me at next Wednesday's service."

"I'll be there."

At exactly 1:00 p.m., Pastor Caldwell announced in a gentle voice that it was time to go in. Arlene and I took our appropriate place, right behind Pastor Caldwell, and we walked into the church side by side. The congregation stood and acknowledged our presence as we entered the sanctuary. Walking in, my eyes focused at the back of Pastor Caldwell's head.

Avoiding eye contact with anyone helped me evade their sorrow. Seeing their pain would have added to my burden and I had more than enough of my own.

The church was so packed that some had to sit in the overflow section. Arlene and I took our seats on the first row, which was reserved for immediate family. The steel gray casket was about ten feet to our right, decorated with beautiful maroon flowers. As A&M's school colors, Arlene wanted everything to reflect Nic's love of his university. The program was designed with maroon and, although I didn't see it, Arlene had given the funeral director a Texas A&M tie for Nic to wear during the viewing portion of the service.

Staring at the casket, my eyes filled with tears and I dropped my head to avoid seeing the box that contained the body of my heart and soul. Not wanting to lose it emotionally, in silence I prayed for strength to hold it together.

Torrey, the funeral director, noticed my anxiety right away and came to my aid until everyone was seated. If the schedule was strictly adhered to, I could survive an hour or so.

Pastor Caldwell welcomed everyone and read a scripture deemed appropriate for funerals. My hearing was fine, but neither the scripture nor his encouraging words registered. Stuck on his opening statement, I couldn't get past, "Welcome to Nicolis Williams' Home Going Service."

The only home where Nic belonged was his Sugar

Land home. Pastor Caldwell went on to name the guests schedule to speak, Ms. Dodie, Gabby House, Floyd LeBlanc, Pastor Walker, and Rep. Charlie Howard.

The speakers all sat on the first row to my extreme right, next to one another. As each speaker completed their talk, the next one rose to recite theirs. A seasoned politician, Rep. Howard took a more high profile position to deliver his message. He went to the pulpit where Pastor Caldwell would deliver the eulogy and he looked prepared to speak longer than the allotted two or three minutes.

He acknowledged Pastor Caldwell and thanked him for the opportunity. He mentioned his own personal tragedy regarding the loss of his son many years ago. He said, "Where are our children? Nico is not in that casket. He's with the Lord. The Word says absent from the body, present with the Lord."

He talked about our first conversation and how typical people in my position want consoling and answers to why, but I didn't want any of those things. "Greg wanted to know, what can we do to prevent another family from experiencing this tragedy again."

He continued, "In 2009, the Texas Legislature passed the Jamie Schanbaum act that required all freshmen who lived in a dorm to be vaccinated against meningitis. We're going to change that law. We can take care of that. That's my job!"

The audience erupted with applause like we were at a political rally. They clapped nonstop with encouragement and appreciation for the commitment he just made.

Pastor Caldwell's strategy worked! Rep. Howard was on the record now for ensuring the law would be modified requiring all students to be vaccinated.

Rep. Howard quoted a scripture for the congregation to consider.

For now we see only a reflection as in a mirror; then we shall see face to face. Now I know in part; then I shall know fully, even as I am fully known.
1 Corinthians 13:12

Clergyman and many biblical scholars utilize this scripture quite often when attempting to provide an answer to the inexplicable question: "Why?"

Rep. Howard's interpretation of the scripture suggests that at this point in our lives we can only see in part. Further, as humans, we cannot see from God's perspective, which can leave us confused and angry. In some instances, we lose faith.

The good news is, when we meet God face to face, all questions of 'why' shall be answered.

Rep. Howard finished his talk by assuring us, "We don't know why Nic's life wasn't spared, but we do know God gave his son to the world so we all could have an everlasting life."

Rep. Howard's brief but well-delivered message meant a lot to me and from the applause of the audience, it touched their hearts as well. He was the perfect prelude to the next and final speaker.

Pastor Caldwell thanked all the participants, and before he began his message he spoke briefly about Nic. "This is a painful moment for me. Nico left us way too early. It was mentioned earlier that someone else at A&M contacted meningitis back in November, so why wasn't something done then? 'Why' can get you stuck! Nico was young, brilliant, personable, God-loving, handsome, and he died from a illness that could have been prevented. What do we do and how do we do it? Greg, Arlene, and Tiffany, I offer you a 'Go Forward Plan'."

His plan consisted of three steps, and the first was entitled "Live Life." His message was from 2 Samuel 12:17-23. King David was fasting and praying for his dying son, but the baby soon died anyway. David's servants were afraid to inform him of his son's death for fear of how he would respond. When David inquired about his son, they told him he died. But to the servants' surprise, David arose from the ground, washed, anointed himself, put on fresh clothes, and went to church to worship God.

Pastor Caldwell used these scriptures as an example of how we should respond to Nic's death. When a death occurs, the loss hurts and doesn't go away for some time, but like David, we have to continue to "live life."

"Jesus came so we can have life and have it more abundantly. A very good example of continuing to live life is a decision the Williams family made. Five people are alive today because Nico's organs were donated."

Extended applause from that acknowledgement made me feel much better about our decision.

The one thing I missed most about attending Windsor Village is Pastor Caldwell's comedic remarks during his sermons.

After mentioning Nic's cremation, he said, "I know a lot of you are shocked and dismayed by that decision. You believe Nico will need his body in heaven, so why would the family make such a decision. The same God that gave him this body is the same God that can give him a new body."

He assured everyone their spirits go to heaven and everything else stays right here. "Your weaves, your extensions, and your underwear, they all stay right here."

Everyone in the sanctuary cracked up laughing.

His second point of the Go Forward Plan was to "Kill Death," from the same scripture above. It's quite natural to grief the loss of a loved one, but you must avoid getting bogged down within that grief. You gotta kill the thoughts associated with their death.

"Self-pity; Dead. If I coulda, shoulda, woulda; Dead. If only; Dead."

He encouraged us to associate with like-minded friends and family. Too many times, people who mean well accompany our grief, but their message is more of a pity party than encouragement.

The last point of the Plan was to "Forge Forward."

As difficult as it may be when losing someone, we have to move forward.

"Go when you don't feel like going. Don't let today find you in the same spot as yesterday."

To make his point, he took a few steps, simulating being stuck in mud, yet he pushed forward. He returned to the scripture, "After David learned of his son's death, he cleaned himself up that moment and went to church at the very time when critics said he should abandon God."

That point really hit home. David went to church and worshiped because he loved God unconditionally.

Pastor Caldwell ended his message by quoting Viktor Frankl, the author who wrote the book, *The Meaning of Life*.

"If you have a WHAT to live for, then you can make it through any HOW."

The pallbearers were called to their positions around the casket and we followed them as they led the procession out of the church.

After they loaded the casket into the hearse, I stopped, placed my hand on it, and whispered "Goodbye, my son, until we meet again."

CHAPTER 11
BATTLE

Do not conform any longer to the pattern of this world, but be transformed by the renewing of your mind. Then you will be able to test and approve what God's will is... his good, pleasing and perfect will.
Romans 12:2

That scripture was my son's favorite bible verse. I had no idea until one of his friends referred to it on his Facebook page. After I studied the scripture for hours and tried to interpret its meaning, the following thought came to my mind: Don't follow the traditional way of processing Nic's death by grieving and soul-searching for answers. Instead, trust God, allow him to lead me, and by doing so, the will of God will be revealed. Changing the law was the clear purpose, but getting there would be a monumental challenge.

Though very early in the process, I was convinced something larger than life was taking shape. Sitting on the sideline and watching it happen wasn't an option. Unsure of my role and having no idea what I was getting myself into, I felt God was leading me on a journey where only he knew the final destination.

At first I was alone, but by my obedience, the appropriate people would appear at the right place and time to assist me every step of the way. For certain, God was interceding, but why now and not before?

Like a reoccurring migraine, the "Why?" question kept coming back.

Remembering Pastor Caldwell's message about 'the way "Why" can get you stuck!' I let it go. Nic was gone and there was no point trying to comprehend the incomprehensible. My only concern was fulfilling the destiny of my journey by changing the meningitis law to include all students.

Changing the law would fulfill the purpose that Nic's death wasn't in vain and it was more than an unlucky random occurrence. Nicolis "Nico" Terrel Williams lived on this earth for twenty years and his life influenced in a positive way everyone who was fortunate enough to know him. I was determined his death would have even more impact for those who would never have the pleasure of meeting him. If successful, all Texas college students would forever benefit from Nic's sacrifice.

The funny thing is, he always told me he would be famous one day. In an ironic twist of fate, he was right. I just wish it could have been by any other means than his death.

Creating or modifying a law in Texas is quite a

convoluted process and provides ample opportunities for defeat before it reaches the Governor's desk for approval. The document is identified as a bill and it travels through the treacherous legislative minefield until the Governor executes it, at which point it then becomes a law. The legislative process is a definite cure for insomnia, so the details are excluded from this book on purpose. Just know it's similar to an obstacle course and with every accomplishment the next obstacle becomes more challenging.

To further complicate the process, unexpected trap doors await the bill, or even a knife-wielding legislator eager to pay back a political debt will kill the bill. Sponsors of a bill gather support from various professional associations, expert witnesses, and public support. Sometimes indisputable studies are used to convince legislators to support their agenda.

At every step of the process, opponents of a bill pull out all stops to defeat it, if in their perception, it's not in the best interest of the public.

Prior to speaking with Rep. Howard, my only involvement in the political process was casting votes in presidential elections. That one conversation thrust me into the ruthless world of politics and dead center of a political firestorm concerning public health. I needed a crash course to understand the legislative process, government's role in public health, and the very polarizing issue of vaccines. Alone in a foreign land, I had no one to turn to for help. Little did I know, but a cavalry of well-informed professionals were on their way to assist me and provide all the ammunition necessary to secure a victory.

After the home going service, an avalanche of people who earnestly wanted to assist with my quest of modifying the meningitis law blindsided me. By granting all interview requests with radio, newspapers, magazines, and television stations, I made sure the public was well informed of Nic's tragic story and how easily his death could be repeated by any college student anywhere in America. The message really resonated with people, but at the time, I had no idea the positive impact those interviews would have on my mission.

Nic's very preventable death not only destroyed our world, but it touched the hearts of everyone who knew him and countless others who didn't. Lots of people were encouraged to act. Anything was better than just accepting what happened as fate or bad luck. Whether it was divine intervention, coincidence, or just maybe the stars in perfect alignment, the ensuing support was as unpredictable as Nic's death, and yet, so very inspirational.

Just days after the funeral, a chain of events was put in motion and resources became available that created an impenetrable path leading all the way to the Governor's desk.

Of the many phone calls I received, three women of note played a significant role with my legislative education. Anna Dragsbaek of The Immunization Partnership (TIP), Frankie Miley of Meningitis

Angels, and Patsy Shanbaum of the J.A.M.I.E. Group are all advocates of immunization awareness, and they played a significant role in creating the current meningitis law. Their help and the assistance from many others would be required to the fight the political opponent known as the anti-immunization community.

When Anna called and reintroduced herself, at first I didn't recall speaking with her before, but when she mentioned Methodist Hospital, the memories returned right away. Anna was very instrumental in putting us in contact with the doctors regarding the failed transfer. After explaining my involvement with Rep. Howard, she described the purpose of her organization and how we could work together in hopes of changing the law.

I owe a huge debt of gratitude to Anna for her leadership and her compassion, and for being the lightning rod to get things done. Without her organizational skills, political savvy, and determination, we didn't stand a chance of success. She explained in detail the challenges we would face and who the players were, both for and against us. She also made it very clear that I would play a major role in convincing the legislators that a change in the law would without doubt save the lives of college students throughout Texas.

Anna developed a very strategic and calculated plan that we hoped would garner sufficient legislative support to guarantee us a victory. This new law would be a significant accomplishment for the state of Texas and even more so for the immunization community nationwide. For the first time since receiving Rep. Howard's call, I had an idea of what God's plan entailed and my participation within it.

Almost overnight, a team of highly knowledgeable professionals and supporters were available for my assistance. As my education developed, doors were now open that had been previously closed. Influential politicians made themselves available, powerful community leaders offered their assistance, the medical community backed us one hundred percent, special interest groups were highly supportive, and victims of meningitis stood by, ready and willing to aid us in any way they could.

In addition to the team of professionals, we were encouraged to a great degree by a recommendation from The Center for Disease Control. They recently changed a position held for many years and now recommend a meningitis booster at 16 years of age for ALL adolescences. This change was significant because a booster at that age would protect adolescents throughout the period they're most susceptible. With such an "array of punches" at our disposal, modifying the law would be as easy as Rocky Balboa taking on Pee Wee Herman.

Who would oppose protecting college students against a heinous disease that dismembers bodies and sometimes kills its victims within a matter of hours? Who in their right mind would oppose preventing unnecessary hardships for families of meningitis victims? Who?

Unbeknownst to me, achieving my goal would grow much more difficult than I first thought.

The anti-immunization community was a very threatening opponent capable of delivering their own knockout punch. Their consistent message and goal was to persuade the legislature that government had no right forcing its citizens to immunize against meningitis or any other disease. The anti-vaccine movement is very active throughout the country and presents a significant threat to controlling the spread of contagious diseases. Scores of passionate people believe vaccines can cause conditions like autism, along with other severe physical and mental abnormalities. Many physicians and celebrities support their beliefs, but no scientific proof confirms any of their outrageous claims.

The anti-vaxxers, as they are more commonly known, have a right to their opinions, but their position is without merit because it lacks substantiated medical research. No doubt, adverse reactions have occurred with vaccines, but those are very rare, and, in most cases patients may experience a fever or sore arm where the vaccine was administered.

The fervent anti-vaxxers are convinced that vaccines are harmful, just as the medical community is unequivocally convinced that vaccines save lives.

So, who's right?

The one ace in the hole we had was scientific

evidence, which should trump any claims based on word-of-mouth, Google searches, and celebrity endorsements. Would the legislators do what was in the best interest of their constituents and of the state, or would they support the anti-vaxxers to avoid a public display of controversy created by the overzealous group. Science vs. Speculation.

The heavyweight fight was on, with the clock ticking. The 82nd Texas Legislative Session would end May 30, and we had approximately 85 days remaining to get the bill passed. If successful, all college students and their families would be protected from the sufferings and ravages of bacterial meningitis.

The dedicated team with whom I worked knew very well what we were up against and each obstacle to overcome. All the political maneuvering and strategizing was alien to me, but as a rookie oblivious of the pending battle, I was willing to do whatever was required to ensure passage of the bill. They welcomed me with tons of support and encouragement. Still grieving from losing Nic and not knowing whether I was going or coming, God was my beacon and I trusted him again.

Our bill was considered highly controversial and thus it presented many more challenges than the routine legislative obstacle course. To avoid the perceived controversy, opportunities for killing the bill rose to an unusual degree. The following were the "opportunities" we faced:

1) The legislative session allows 60 days for introducing bills and Nic died 30 days after the session started. We had 30 days remaining to get the ball rolling or wait two years for the next session.

2) The anti-immunization community was well organized and well connected throughout the state legislature. Although we had scientific evidence and medical experts as witnesses, the anti-vaxxers used other methods to make their point. Without any credible science supporting their position, they raised hell for legislators who opposed them. Many legislators chose to avoid the confrontations by voting in support of the anti-vaxxers, regardless of how questionable their science.

3) The Republican Party was the controlling party during the 82nd Legislature and they were primarily anti-government and very conservative. Our bill opposed the fundamental beliefs of many Republicans, which was less government intrusion into the lives of all Texans. Supporting a bill that required a vaccine could be viewed as a betrayal to their party. Gathering their support was crucial and difficult at best. Without it, we were "down for the count."

4) Texas, like the rest of the nation, was in a recession, so the bill could not include any cost to the State. Talk circulated that, if the legislature passed the bill, it would be considered a mandate, and if so, the State would be required to provide funding for vaccinating all who were affected by the law. If the State were held responsible for funding the mandate, the bill would be dead on arrival.

5) Colleges and universities were reluctant to support the law. Without doubt, the law would create an additional workload to implement the procedures associated with administrating the law. Working in educational procurement my entire career, I understood the reluctance when the State passed a law that increased my workload. Most oppose it at first, but, after a year or two, the increased workload becomes routine and absorbed into the daily responsibilities without much effort.

6) The Supreme Court recently upheld a law that prevents pharmaceutical companies from being sued for vaccine casualties. This was a mother lode of evidence for the anti-vaxxers. The Supreme Court's decision provided justification why the State should

not force immunization on its citizens. If they did and, God forbid, a casualty occurred, the pharmaceutical company had no liability and the family had no recourse.

7) Governor Perry would likely veto the bill. This was particularly threatening because of what occurred during the 2007 legislative session. Gov. Perry signed an executive order requiring all girls entering the 6th grade to be vaccinated against the human papillomavirus (HPV), the most common sexually transmitted disease and the principal cause of cervical cancer. He took a beating from the general public, fellow legislators, and concerned parents all across the country. The negative response was so overwhelming the legislators passed H.B. 1098 to override Gov. Perry's executive order. He could have used his veto power to kill the bill and allow his executive order to remain intact, but he wisely chose not to do it.

Even though that scenario took place four years before Nic died, we were very concerned that Gov. Perry's experience would lead him to veto any immunization legislation that crossed his desk. With some talk of his running for president, the whole negative HPV experience was sure to be a huge target on his back for his opponents. If the rumor were correct, why would he take a chance of alienating the public again by supporting another immunization law? Regardless of his position, it was a chance we had to take. We certainly had a difficult fight ahead of us and at times, I wondered which group represented Pee Wee Herman. Either way, I trusted that with God, all things are possible.

What then shall we say in response to these things? If God is for us, who can be against us.
Romans 8:31

CHAPTER 12

PROMISE

Often times during a highly emotional setting, commitments are made with the knowledge that the likelihood of fulfilling a promise is suspect at best. Individuals making a commitment feel a moral obligation to deliver some form of restitution to the suffering party. Their intentions are sincere and driven by the urgency to do what's right, but unfortunately, politics can suppress the best of good intentions.

We see this played out all too often after a mass shooting and the public demands something be done about our country's gun laws. Congressional leaders and the president are quick to respond, but fail to deliver any meaningful legislation. The blame game is played, the public's safety continues to be at risk, and the scenario is repeated when another mass shooting occurs.

Elements of that scenario were ever so present in our situation and the same result was a definite possibility. Granted, so many variables have to be considered when passing legislation that affects public health, but if lives will be saved as a result, how could any reasonable person be in opposition?

Politics, plain and simple! Legislation can solve many of society's ills, but you can't legislate against stupidity. Our success was heavily dependent on Rep. Howard's commitment and his political weight to help him work the system.

We were off to a good start after receiving word he filed House Bill 1816 before the deadline and it was assigned to the House's Public Health Committee. One of his staffers called to inform me of the news and they also suggested I prepare a testimony for the hearing that would be scheduled soon. The legislative baton was passed to me and addressing the Public Health Committee was my first official assignment.

Inside my head, the idea of speaking to the committee made me nauseous. Outwardly, I was ecstatic about the news. We were on our way and confidently guarded about our chances. Even so, my insecurities of public speaking and being the central figure pushed the limits of my comfort zone.

Avoiding attention is a dominant characteristic of my personality and I'm more than comfortable playing a "behind the scenes" role. Since I had no way to avoid addressing the committee, plus knowing my testimony would be crucial in convincing them, fear wasn't an option. Regardless of my perceived shortcomings, I had to "Forge Forward," as Pastor Caldwell so eloquently reminded us during Nic's service.

I called my trusted lifeline, Anna, to tell her the good news and of course, she was way ahead of me. She knew about the House Bill filing and was excited to suggest some tips for my pending testimony.

Without fail, the public hearing was scheduled for March 16, 9:00 a.m., at the state capitol building in Austin, Texas. Anna briefed me on what to expect from the hearing and she was really concerned about my ability to speak to the committee.

People in my position—parents who recently lost their child—often break down in tears in front of the committee and they can't complete their testimony. It's a hard thing to witness for all parties and your heart goes out to the parent, but the hearing must proceed.

Still an emotional wreck, I felt Anna's concern was justified. Who wouldn't be? But I assured Anna that nothing would stop me from addressing the committee, not my insecurities, my fear of public speaking, or my fragile emotional state of mind.

Before the hearing, she asked to review my testimony to see the points I intended to make. I trusted her to the nth degree to be honest with me if I strayed too much from the focal point. The hearing was our first obstacle of a long journey and everything had to be perfect if we were going to be successful.

Anna read it and said my words moved her to tears. She recommended no changes.

I was ready.

For the two-hour drive from Houston to Austin,

Arlene and I planned on leaving around 5:30 a.m. to ensure we wouldn't arrive late and to allow extra time for any potential traffic issues. When we met again at the same Walmart parking lot, every memory came flooding back the moment I parked the car. Not even a month had passed since Nic's funeral, and yet there we were again, meeting to take care of his business.

Unlike the first time, I wasn't powerless or unprepared for what awaited us. I couldn't save my son on our initial trip, but I'd be damned if anything would stop me this time from creating a legacy in his honor. My testimony would be compelling and persuasive enough for a unanimous vote out of the Public Health Committee.

Maybe it was the early morning hours or the unforgiving grief, but dead silence returned as our constant companion. The darkness of the night and quiet confines of our vehicle did little to subdue my anxiety. Drinking four cups of coffee was supposed to keep me awake for the drive, but they also elevated my nerves.

All during the drive, my self-doubt went into overdrive. What in the world was I doing addressing a state hearing? How many people would be in the audience and whom did they represent? Would my message be received as I intended? Would I have an emotional moment? If I did, could I compose myself? What if I missed a word or skipped an entire sentence as I read my testimony? What if I lost my place and used the dreaded... uhhhhh?

After hours of battling my self-esteem issues, we arrived at the state capitol building. Of the many pictures I saw of it throughout my life, none did justice to the massive pink granite structure, which supports the myth that everything is bigger in Texas. The grand old building was intimidating and I felt miserable, inadequate, and out of place due to my disdain for politics.

Our elected officials gather there biannually to make laws that affect all Texas residents, and my opinion of them has always been nothing less than skeptical. I grouped them on a par with salespeople I'd come to loathe after years of listening to sales pitches designed to convince me to buy something I didn't need.

Their true loyalty rested with special interest groups who funded their campaigns and provide luxuries to ensure their loyalty. The constituents they represent are a vital necessity, but they can be manipulated or "sold a bag of goods," thereby keeping us convinced that politicians have our best interests at heart. Further, they are quite skilled at telling people what they want to hear, but never committing to anything.

Rep. Howard appeared to be the very opposite of my biased views and, because of his commitment at Nic's funeral, I believed in him. I hoped and prayed my cynicism of politicians was not justified, at least in my case.

We parked the car at a nearby garage and walked

two blocks to the capitol building. One can't approach the building without noticing the Goddess of Liberty, which sits atop the capitol and watches over the grounds. As we entered the perimeter from the east side, we walked past several giant oak trees that seemed to have a history all to themselves. You could almost hear the leaves whispering stories of Texas' political folklore. Several statues of famous Texans from the past demanded our attention, but we couldn't afford to be late, so we proceeded without reading their plaques describing their contributions to the state.

As we walked passed the restricted vehicle entrance, I overheard voices that grabbed my attention. Several school buses were parked along the capitol streets and at least ten elementary school classes were gathered under the century-old trees. One passionate teacher was telling her class that the capitol building belonged to them and all the citizens of Texas.

That statement struck a nerve and I all of a sudden realized I had no reason to feel afraid or undeserving. As a law-abiding citizen and reluctant taxpayer, I had every right to stand before the legislature and be heard. After all, my commitment to completing God's plan was much stronger than my fear associated with public speaking.

Nic's legacy depended on my ability to overcome my insecurities and, as an added motivation, the lives of future college students were at stake as well.

We entered the capitol building through the tallest doors I had ever walked through. At least 25 feet high, the myth continued. We passed through the security screening station and I stood in awe of what I saw. The artful millwork used in the immense corridors displayed beauty and elegance that gave the building a touch of southern hospitality.

Upon entering the rotunda, I couldn't help but to look up and pause at the beauty of the historic building. Terrazzo tile displays the six flags that have flown over Texas. A white marble statue of Stephen F. Austin greets visitors in the capitol's south foyer. The intricate details of the masonry and wood trimming were all breathtaking.

As we walked around and waited for our escort, we took a minute to view all the portraits of governors who filled the state's highest office. I was surprised to see Ann Richards wasn't the first woman elected governor in Texas. My high school history teacher would have been embarrassed for me. Miriam Ferguson was the first woman to hold that honor back in 1925. The impressive sights distracted me from my fears and my purpose for being in the building, but not for long.

Our escort arrived at about 8:45. "Mr. & Mrs. Williams, I presume?"

"Yes, we are."

"Hi, my name is Jason Sabo and I am extremely honored to meet you both. I work with Anna Dragsbaek by guiding her through the intricacies of legislative process."

When Jason mentioned Anna, I took that to mean he was a lobbyist like my buddy, Stud. Although Jason was dressed in a nice suit and tie, he was as country as country could get. He had a slight Texas twang in his voice, cowboy boots—a Texas standard—and, like many Texans, he uses metaphors to get his point across.

Before approaching us, I overheard him tell someone, "You're slick as goose crap."

I'd never heard that one before, but the description reminded me of my grandparent's farm and I remembered just how slippery goose crap really was.

"Hi, Jason, it's nice to meet you, and any friend of Anna's is a friend of ours."

He continued his introduction, "I offer my deepest sympathies for your loss of your son. As a father of two, words will never adequately express what I would like to say, so please just know how sorry I am and how profoundly inspired I am that, through the pain, you have chosen to fight to improve public policies in our state. Thanks to your efforts and the memory of your son, lives are already being changed and saved."

"Thank you, Jason. Our son shouldn't have been a meningitis victim and we're here to do whatever we can to prevent this tragedy from repeating. I only wish the original bill had the support to include all students, like we seem to have now."

"As do I, Mr. Williams, as do I. Now, we have to

get you two to the hearing room. Please come with me."

We followed Jason down a flight of stairs and through brief hallways that were home to pictures of the State's history and the construction of the building. After going through what seemed like a maze of historical artifacts, we reached an area that was a pleasant surprise.

Emerging from the past into the future, I found it hard to imagine we were in the same building. The lower floors were much more modernized and more suited for the activities of this day and time. The underground floors included a cafeteria, a bookstore, and much better restrooms. We entered what's called a hearing room and Jason took us to a table near the entrance door. There, I completed a brief form that required my name, my affiliation, the bill I was interested in, my support or opposition of the bill, and my intent to speak or not.

In any other circumstance, I would have checked the "not to speak" box, but this occasion was far more compelling than any speaking opportunity ever presented before. This time, I was destined to speak. I felt more than an obligation to speak on Nic's behalf. God's will and the health of future college students depended on me.

We arrived a little early, so there were ample seats available. The pecan-stained wood walls and high-back leather chairs resembled a courtroom, with the exception of no desk for the prosecution or defense. Instead of one chair for a judge, eleven seats were arranged all behind a desk-high partition. Five seats on either side were reserved for the committee members with the chairperson seated in the center.

Their positions were noticeably elevated, compelling any speaker to look up when addressing the committee. I assume this was by design to create a distance and perhaps to intimidate any speaker. The State Seal of Texas hung behind the chairperson in between the Texas and United States flags. The room appeared to seat about 50 to 60 people, with some standing room in the back near the door.

After completing the form, I turned to face the room and tried to imagine the discussions that would take place when the hearing started. By doing so, my anxiety increased ten-fold at the mere thought of taking center stage and speaking to the committee. My fear was bad enough, but I added insult to injury by sweating through my sleeves at my armpits. I could muster no explanation of my perceived panic, but for me, this was equivalent to addressing the United States Supreme Court.

Nothing could be further from the truth, but my mind was convinced. Before leaving home that morning, I looked up a bible verse on courage and saved it on my cell phone, just in case. Prior to taking another step, I felt an overwhelming calmness after reading the following scripture:

Have not I commanded you? Be strong and coura-

geous. Do not be afraid; do not be discouraged, for the LORD your God will be with you wherever you go.
Joshua 1:9

Arlene was already seated and waived me over when Jason approached from behind. "Mr. Williams."

Looking over my shoulder and noticing he wasn't alone, I turned completely around to face him and his guest. "Jason, we're friends, so it's plain ole Greg."

Smiling, he continued, "Okay, Greg it is. Well, Greg, I have someone who wants to meet you. This is Anna Dragsbaek of The Immunization Partnership."

After having so many phone conversations, I felt a huge relief to meet Anna at last. Her stature was about 5'1" at best, yet the height of her intelligence and passion reached the stars. The compassion projected from her dark eyes revealed medical horrors she experienced as a Peace Corps volunteer in Sierra Leone, West Africa. Anna can only be described as a true professional with a drive and tenacity to accomplish the impossible. She may not always get her way with legislators, but they know she's thoroughly informed and extremely knowledgeable. I was thrilled to have her on our team.

"Greg, it's such an honor to meet you. After all our conversations, it's nice to place a face with the voice. How are you?"

"I'm good, Anna. A little nervous but, I'm fine."

"That's a good thing. It's perfectly normal to be a little nervous. It helps keep you on your toes."

"I sure hope so. I'm aiming to score some big points today."

"No doubt, you will. We don't have much time, but there are couple of people I really want you to meet."

We walked a short distance across the room where Anna introduced me to two other members of our team. "Greg, these are the two very courageous women I've been telling you about, Patsy and Jamie Schanbaum. They will be testifying today along with you and several others."

"Good morning, ladies. It's a pleasure to meet you both. Anna has told me so much about you two that it feels like we're related."

Patsy is of Hispanic heritage with long black hair and an angelic smile that could lure any man of her choice. As a single woman in her mid-fifties, she was in great shape and probably broke lots of hearts throughout her lifetime. By the fine toned muscles of her calves, it was obvious she's an avid runner or an exercise junkie.

Of the two ladies, Patsy spoke first. "I feel the same way, Greg, but I hate we had to meet under these circumstances. It's a shame what happened to your son, but he's the reason why we're here today. We hope his situation will get the legislature's attention and the law will be modified to include all students."

"I couldn't agree more. It would be a nice legacy for Nic, but even more so, innocent lives would be saved."

The missing fingers from Jamie's hands were hard to ignore, but I attempted not to look. She walked towards me without a hint of awkwardness from the prosthetics she seemed to have mastered. Bacterial meningitis had caused the amputation of her legs just below her knees and several of her fingers. A beautiful young lady, she possessed a cunning smile that suggested she couldn't possibly be guilty, but was. Not a spitting image of her mother, but she carried the same youthful gene. With no trouble they could pass for sisters.

I could only imagine the pain and horror Jamie must have gone through when the bacterium ravaged her body. The physical pain was harsh enough, but the mental anguish of losing one's limbs penetrates much deeper and the mirror never lets you forget.

My heart went out to her and I wanted to offer some encouraging words, but I didn't know her well enough. She went through hell, but the good news is, she made it. God has a purpose for her life and I hope she doesn't allow the setback to stop or define her.

We extended our arms to shake hands, but I changed course and decided to hug her instead. Not certain if my last second switch was because she survived her attack and I wanted to acknowledge support for her, or if I detected a kindred connection between her and Nic and hugging her was like hugging him.

"And how are you today, young lady?"

"Oh, I'm a little antsy. I have class today, so I

hope the hearing won't take too long."

"Well, I hope it's over soon, too. We're very thankful for your being here today and sharing your story once again. It must be difficult telling it over and over."

"To be honest, I've told it so many times, it really doesn't bother me at all."

"Really? You're a brave young woman and I admire you more than you could imagine."

Her shrewd smile reappeared as Rep. Howard approached us. "Good morning, Greg, the hearing is about to start and I just wanted to say hi to you and Ms. Williams and also to thank you again for your courage. I will not be able to stay through the hearing, but I wanted to address the committee before leaving."

Rep. Howard was a longtime member of the legislature and carried considerable influence among his colleagues. At his request, the committee moved HB1816 (The Meningitis Bill) to the top of the agenda and saved us hours of sitting and waiting for the Bill to be debated.

Dressed in a tailored navy suit, white shirt, and patriotic red tie, Rep. Howard resembled a CFO of a Fortune 500 organization. A slender man in his mid-sixties, he exemplified class and professionalism.

"Good morning, sir. Thank you for keeping your word and for everything you're doing to see this bill get through."

"This is just the first step, Greg, and we have a

few more hurdles to overcome, but we'll get it done, I promise."

Not as confident as Rep. Howard and, even though I felt God's presence, I still had doubts.

"Good morning, everyone. The House Public Health Committee is now in session," announced the Chairperson.

As everyone settled in their seats, a still calmness resonated within me. The room was filled to capacity and my normal anxiety would already be escalating with the anticipation of addressing an audience. After scanning the room, I had no way to determine who supported the bill and who opposed it. Anna advised me there definitely would be opposition and primarily from the anti-vaxxers. They exhibited no distinctive body language, so identifying them was impossible.

But then I thought, why should I give a hoot? Prepared, prayed-up, and having a profound purpose, I cared less about who was in attendance. Above all else, God's presence calmed my fears and arrested my anxiety attack.

The Chairperson announced a change in the agenda and informed us that HB 1816 would be heard first. She read a brief summary of the Bill and then introduced Rep. Howard as the author of the bill and provided him an opportunity to speak to the committee.

"Good morning, Chairperson Kolkhorst and committee members. Thank you for rearranging the agenda and placing HB 1816 as your first item to be discussed. I authored this bill because I feel very strongly that all college students should be protected against meningitis. As you know, the Williams family recently lost their son Nicolis due to the disease. Before the funeral of their son, Greg contacted me and he was very concerned about preventing this situation from ever happening again. Their concern for others at such a horrible time made a lasting impression on me.

"The current law requires only college students living in a dorm to be vaccinated. Because Nicolis didn't live in a dorm, he wasn't required to be vaccinated and thus resulted in his very preventable death. This bill will modify the law and require all first-time college students to be vaccinated. Students are our future. They are our hope and we need to protect them in every way we can. I urge the committee to pass this bill out of committee. Thank you."

Rep. Howard returned to his seat after addressing the committee. As he spoke, I had observed body language of the committee members, which told me they considered him a much-respected member of the House. I couldn't be more pleased that Rep. Howard represented Nic. His confidence and demeanor suggested he had significant pull with his fellow legislators and if so, the bill stood a good chance of a favorable vote.

Chairperson Kolkhorst then called Jamie to testify. She approached the podium and exchanged pleasantries with the committee as if she knew them all in person.

In some ways she did. If they didn't know Jamie as an individual, they all knew her story and her courage in convincing the 2009 legislature to pass the current meningitis law. Jamie's case received tons of media attention and, with her willingness to exhibit how the disease devastated her body, she made an overwhelming impact on everyone who listened.

Unlike me, she didn't have any notes or papers to share with the committee. She was accustomed to speaking to a committee of its stature without fear or preparation. Jamie spoke about that unforgettable evening when preparing to attend a party and suddenly falling ill. She decided to delay going for a while and rest a bit. Later, when she attempted to get out of bed by placing her feet on the floor, she experienced excruciating pain. Right away she called her sister, who rushed her to the hospital where she was diagnosed with bacterial meningitis.

The disease spread very quickly through her blood and the doctors were helpless to stop it. To save her, they had to amputate her legs and several fingers. She mentioned how, in a matter of hours, her blood stopped circulating to those parts of her body and they were essentially dead and had to be removed.

Jamie ended her testimony by saying, "One day, I was a typical college student enjoying my life and planning on dancing the night away at a party. The very next day, instead of being exhausted from dancing, my legs were amputated from a meningitis attack. As tragic as my case was, I'm one of the lucky ones. I'm here today because another college student wasn't as lucky. I ask you to pass this bill to protect all Texas college students from what happened to me and Nicolis Williams."

She thanked the committee and returned to her seat. You could hear a pin drop on cotton. She was poised, elegant, decisive, and effective in knowing when and how to make points with the committee. A couple of members thanked her for her courage and for taking part in the hearing.

Clueless to when my name would be called, my nerves were not as rattled as they have always been when speaking in public. Maybe my comfort was due to the speech I would read instead of "talking from the cuff." Reading was a necessity because I couldn't afford to miss any key points with the committee. The speech was prepared about a week earlier, timed to perfection for the allotted three minutes per speaker.

Reading the scripture once more assured a peace within me that was as unusual as my addressing a committee of state legislators. Chairperson Kolkhorst called my name, "Greg Williams, in support of the bill."

The room fell quiet. I rose to my feet and approached the podium. The walk was only about eight feet, yet it felt much farther. Everything seemed to happen in slow motion. My unhurried stride felt long, the blink of my eyes took seconds, and just raising my head to address the committee was a measured movement. As I settled in my seat, the timer started and time resumed its regular pace.

"Good morning, Madam Chair and Public Health Committee Members. Thank you and Rep. Howard for allowing me an opportunity to speak with you this morning.

"Because my son can't speak for himself, I'd like to take this time to share with you the tragic circumstances that led to his untimely death. On February 8th, I received a phone call that devastated my life forever. I was informed that my son, Nic, was diagnosed with bacterial meningitis and we needed to get to College Station immediately. We arrived at the hospital about 4:00 p.m., three hours after receiving the initial phone call. The doctors told us Nic was brought to the hospital by ambulance, was tested for meningitis, and within eight minutes after arrival, he fell unconscious. Approximately three hours later, we were told Nic suffered a brain aneurysm and that his brain was swollen to the point that no further treatment was available.

"In essence, we were told he was brain dead.

"Because my family and I are Christians and we believe in the healing power of God, we prayed for a miracle. Prayers and support came pouring in from all around the country. Unfortunately, Nic died three days later.

"I have no words to adequately describe the pain

and sorrow we feel from the loss of our only son and sibling. In less than 24 hours, Nic went from a very healthy and vibrant young man with a tremendous future ahead of him to a brain dead invalid. We were in shock because something like this just wasn't supposed to happen.

"We had so many questions and no response made sense. How did he contract the virus? Are there others infected? Wasn't he vaccinated against this and other diseases? Why didn't A&M notify us of the earlier meningitis case on campus?

"Our grief became unbearable when we discovered that Nic was not required to get vaccinated because he didn't live in a dorm. As you know, the current law only requires freshmen who live in a dorm to be vaccinated. Because Texas A&M didn't have any available dorm rooms when my son was accepted, he was forced to live off campus. He and thousands of students across this state are at risk of contracting a heinous bacterium that mutilates or kills within hours.

"The current law is incomplete and leaves too many students exposed to an untimely death or disfigurement. It's like having a seat belt law that requires only the driver to buckle up. Aren't the lives of the passengers just as important as the driver? In comparison, shouldn't all college students be vaccinated against meningitis regardless of where they live?

"If HB1816 becomes law, no college student in

Texas will be subject to the devastation this bacteria causes and no parent will have to suffer the loss of their beloved child. I can only imagine that the original law left such a huge gap to accommodate the opposition to mandatory vaccinations. I suppose their position is: the occurrences of a meningitis attack are too rare to justify mandatory immunization.

"My response to that position would be: What does the magic number have to be? How many students should die or be disfigured before the number is justifiable? Or better yet, if it were their child, what position would they take?

"I guarantee you no parent wants to bury their child and they would do anything to preserve their life. That's why I'm standing before you today as an advocate for all future college students and their parents.

"Some believe students should have a choice of taking the vaccine or not. During my son's funeral, over 200 students attended who were in close contact with him. They were asked to raise their hands if they had taken the vaccine. Only a few raised their hands. Because meningitis always happens to someone else or because young adults believe they're invincible, many are convinced that something so horrible just can't happen to them. I'm sure my son thought likewise. To protect our students, don't give them a choice.

"It's spring break for thousands of students throughout Texas. This week, many college students will be enjoying themselves with spring break activities or visiting home to catch up with family and friends. Sadly, my son won't be doing either. To prevent families from enduring our suffering and to ensure their love ones will return home safely, I beg you and your colleagues to pass HB 1816. Thank you for your time and consideration."

Before I turned to take my seat, Chairperson Kolkhorst called my name. "Mr. Williams, I'm so sorry for your loss. I know how difficult this must be for you and your family and I applaud you for being here today."

As I thanked her and started towards my seat, Rep. Howard stood up and shook my hand. "Greg, you did a good job".

Although the speech was very brief, it felt like an elephant had been lifted from my shoulders. With no mistakes with my delivery, I beat the three-minute time limit. But I had no immediate way to determine if my speech made an impact with the committee. By not just reading the speech verbatim, I tried to pause at some strategic points and make eye contact with the members. My intent was to create enough empathy for my loss that they could see the logic of supporting the bill.

I thanked Rep. Howard and returned to my seat. Two more supporters of the bill spoke, Frankie Miley and Patsy Schanbaum. Neither speaker had a written statement, which suggested they were accustomed to addressing the committees or they were just comfortable with their message. I hoped to be as comfortable and secure as they were about telling their stories, but I also wished more my services were never needed in the first place.

The Chairperson then called Dawn Richardson. This was the first of the anti-vaxxers who opposed the bill. Dawn is president of Parents Requiring Open Vaccine Education. (P.R.O.V.E.) I grant that it's a creative name and catchy acronym for their organization, but it is also an oxymoron. The "Open Vaccine Education" part of their name suggests a willingness to be objective, yet they reject validated scientific research and accept hearsay as evidence in supporting their eccentric claims.

Most health-related bills passed by the legislature are based on recommendations from the Advisory Committee on Immunization Practices, a division of the Center for Disease Control and Prevention. Medical and public health experts, who also are well aware of the anti-vaxxers' popularity and their cause, make their recommendations. Before going public, they exercise extreme scrutiny to justify their positions.

As the leader of their group, Dawn was not in the same league as Anna. However, she was as effective in persuading some legislators of their anti-vaccine message. The imbedded parenthesis surrounding her mouth and the void of compassion in her eyes had taken its toll from all the years fighting for her purpose. She looked tired and seemed to have a huge chip on her shoulder. After introducing herself to the committee, she made references describing the proposed bill as a machine gun approach to such an isolated and rare event. She quoted bacterial meningitis incidence of occurrence, both nationwide and within Texas.

My own research revealed the following: The Texas Department of State Health Services reported 400 bacterial meningitis cases in 2008, 336 in 2009, and 377 in 2010. Of these totals, it's estimated that 10% affected with the disease would die. If the estimates are correct, 40 people died from bacterial meningitis in 2008, 33 people died in 2009, and 37 in 2010.

PROVE and other anti-vaccine groups believe those deaths are acceptable losses in comparison to general population.

Hearing the term "acceptable losses" was a wake-up call for me, igniting a volcano's eruption of determination that extended throughout every molecule within my body. *How dare she believe Nic's death was an acceptable loss!*

While I will never understand that logic, she and her supporters have a right to believe in it and to defend their beliefs. Every life is a precious gift from God and worthy of every effort in protecting it. 'Acceptable Losses' should never be considered when a life is at stake.

For the first time, I got angry. Real angry. I

couldn't hear the remainder of her testimony because I could not get past her insensitivity to human life. Nevertheless, I tried listening to Dawn's warped sense of rationale and hoped she respected us enough not to say anything negative or specific about Nic.

She mentioned that the hearing was based on a couple of families affected by bacterial meningitis and the numbers don't support any action by the legislature. Restraining myself was a hopeless thought, had she insulted the memory of my son. Thank God, she didn't. She ended her testimony, and then a parent who claimed her daughter was negatively affected by a vaccine spoke next.

The mother of a 12-year-old girl claimed her daughter had a negative reaction to a vaccine, which caused her mental impairment. She mentioned how, within 24 hours of receiving a vaccine, her daughter experienced a very high fever and acted out of character. The doctors eventually got her temperature back to normal, but could give no explanation why her daughter behaved out of the norm. She was very forgetful, she couldn't concentrate on anything for very long, and she appeared to have regressed several years in her mental development. Because the doctors couldn't provide any plausible explanation, the mother researched the situation on her own and determined her daughter experienced a negative reaction to the vaccine.

Was her research flawed or was there some validity to her assertion?

Based on the science of vaccine safety, it's quite unlikely the vaccine caused any of the problems her daughter exhibited. The CDC reports the United States has the safest vaccine supply than it ever had before. It's extremely rare that someone would experience a serious side effect. In most instances, vaccines are perfectly safe, effective with no adverse reactions other than a mild fever or soreness at the point of injection.

Something happened to her daughter; however, without scientific proof that the vaccine caused the problem, it's very difficult to support her position. Still, anyone with a heart couldn't help but feel sympathy for them.

Although I still fumed from Dawn's testimony, I believe the mother's claim warrants a thorough investigation, but not at the expense of HB1816.

For the most part, the committee members allowed the supporters and opponents to speak freely, except at one point during Dawn's testimony. Representative Zerwas, a licensed physician, asked her to validate some of the claims she was making.

Dawn continued to speak, but she avoided answering Dr. Zerwas' question. He repeated his question and asked her to provide some sort of validation to her claims that vaccines caused the medical issues she professed. Again, she evaded his inquiry by quoting some unrelated facts.

He interrupted her and said, "Since you will not answer my question directly, I will consider your testimony irrelevant."

Based on that exchange, I knew we had at least one supporter of the bill. I couldn't read the body language of the members, but they all looked receptive. Because of my past disappointment, however, I wouldn't allow myself to be too confident the bill would pass out of the hearing phase.

When all speakers had completed their testimony, the Committee faced three options: vote to pass the bill out of the committee hearing; reject it, thus killing the bill; or delay the vote until additional information is obtained and reviewed. A "Nay" vote would be a crucial blow, but not a necessarily a knockout punch. If that happened, another legislator from the Senate chamber would have to take up our cause, but time was running out. It was imperative we obtain this first victory and build momentum for the mounting challenges that lay ahead.

After little debate, the Committee decided to delay their vote until more information became available. Needless to say, I felt disappointed.

I had more questions after their decision than before the hearing began. What additional information did they need? Who would be responsible for providing the information? Was it a tactic to kill the bill? How long would the process take before they voted again?

I found it hard to keep a positive outlook after the first setback.

Anna and Rep. Howard spoke with me separately

regarding the committee's decision and each presented their theory of why a vote wasn't taken. The reasons included: the committee wanted to review the recommendations of the Center of Disease Control regarding meningitis vaccinations; they wanted to ensure there would be no cost if the bill became law; and lastly, they wanted to ensure there was a conscientious objection clause included in the bill.

A few days after the hearing, Anna contacted me and confirmed the reason was due to the conscientious objection issue. They insisted the bill had to provide that option to ensure their support.

Anna wanted my opinion and I was unequivocally against it. Giving the students an opportunity to opt out of taking the vaccine would undermine the purpose of the law. What's the logic if, on one hand all freshmen are required to be vaccinated, and on the other hand, they are given an opportunity to opt out. Anna was very concerned about my reaction so she described in detail what the conscientious objection included, hoping to convince me to be more receptive to the idea.

The clause included three reasons that allowed a student to opt out:

(1) students must have a legitimate health concern and be confirmed by a license physician.

(2) students could claim a religious objection to taking vaccines.

(3) if students had a philosophical reason, they could opt out.

Objections 1 & 2 were reasonable and acceptable, but the philosophical reason was very problematic. I had visions of students utilizing that objection to make a mockery of the law. If they wanted to claim their objection based on the fact that the world is round, no one would challenge them and they would be allowed to opt out.

For the first time during the process, I felt a sense of authority, a sense of control in determining whom the bill would impact. My opinion required all incoming freshman to be vaccinated whether they wanted to or not.

Empowered? Yes, but my sense of authority would be short-lived. They consulted me regarding my opinion, but that's where any perceived power, authority, or control came to a screeching halt. When I expressed my "demands" to Rep. Howard, he responded in no uncertain terms: "If you want this bill to go through and become law, the conscientious objection clause must be included. If not, the bill will die. Period."

My first lesson in politics was the act of compromise. If you're not willing, you can't play the game. Anna likes to say, "Politics is like making sausage. You like the outcome, but you don't want to know its ingredients."

I had no real choice in the matter and I surely

wasn't blinded by any self-righteousness. By retreating to my observation role, I allowed the professionals to do their jobs. When asked, I would provide my opinion, but I could offer nothing more than that. They were the salaried players and knew all the potholes to avoid if we were going to achieve the victory we all so desperately wanted. Thankful they considered my opinion, I stayed out of their way from that point on.

Later I discovered the State of Texas allows parents to opt out of all vaccines for the reasons given above. Texas is a conservative state and conservative groups believe vaccine requirements interfere with a parent's right to make medical choices for their children. It didn't make a difference that the people affected by the bill are adults and don't require their parents' consent.

My argument was a moot point and I conceded my position.

Two weeks after the hearing, HB 1816 was amended to include a conscientious objection clause and the Public Health Committee voted unanimously (9-0 with 2 absent) in favor of the bill.

Thank God! We were on our way.

CHAPTER 13

THE MIDAS TOUCH

Every now and then, a superior athlete will exhibit a performance so outstanding that it defies all logical explanation. A basketball point guard shoots with dead-eye precision and makes ten 3-pointers in a row, a football running back eludes tacklers and gains 300 yards in one game, or a baseball pitcher pin-points each pitch and throws a no-hitter. All are rare and exceptional feats of excellence and dominance.

Many athletes describe their dominant performance as "being in a zone." They believe they're unstoppable, and many times their opponents are convinced as well. Their skills are so heightened that they achieve everything they attempt with relative ease. Some refer to the experience as the 'Midas Touch.' In Greek mythology, King Midas was famous for his ability to turn everything he touched into gold.

In reality as well as myth, success is achieved by

having faith in one's ability to do the impossible.

Christians expected the same result when we have faith in God to answer our prayers. We pray and pray in earnest, believing God will respond, yet many times it feels our prayers go unnoticed.

Despite my best efforts, Nic's hospitalization was anything but the "Midas Touch" and none of us had any "Zone" to acknowledge. Every prayer isn't answered according to one's desire because God sees the bigger picture and will respond at the appropriate time and place, with the necessary support.

Even though my faith was rock solid, God didn't answer my prayers. Everything we tried failed. But things were changing.

Having passed the first major hurdle, I was relieved and encouraged by our win. The excitement from our success lifted my spirits until the next obstacle. For me, our triumph was temporary and overshadowed by the constant longing for Nic. Only six weeks had passed since his death and I learned to my great sadness that the ole cliché "time heals all wounds" doesn't apply to a death of one's child. Still feeling trapped in a horrific nightmare, my only rescue would be the sound of Nic calling me Dad once again.

With our first victory behind us and momentum climbing, demands on my time increased three-fold. So much so, I found barely enough time to breathe, let alone mourn Nic's death. Keeping busy was good therapy, so I accommodated all requests. Wallowing in my sorrows wasn't an option, but maybe that was God's plan all along.

We received some excellent news from the Senate chamber. Sen. Wendy Davis filed SB 1107, which was very similar to HB 1816 filed by Rep. Howard. SB 1107 was considered a companion bill, meaning both bills would work their way through their respective chambers at the same time.

This came as terrific news because the legislative session is so short and therefore a companion bill saves considerable time. Without a companion bill, HB 1816 would have to go through the legislative process in the House chamber and then repeat the process in the Senate chamber. Many bills die during this process because the legislative session simply runs out of time.

Soon after the bill was assigned, I received notice that my testimony was required for the Higher Education Committee.

A week before the hearing, Rep. Howard's office contacted me about a petition his office received from Kempner High School, the same school Nic graduated from a few years earlier. The student council had submitted a petition with 500 student signatures, all supporting the new meningitis bill. Unbelievable! No one from the school had contacted us and most of the students didn't even know Nic. Yet they cared enough about a former student to support our efforts with a petition. In all his years in the legislature, Rep. Howard said he never experienced any support from high school students.

The petition was another example of the momentum that seemed to be growing faster than my imagination could fathom. God was turning around a situation fraught with pain and misery and replacing it with his love. I felt an overwhelming outpouring of love and empathy from everyone associated with our quest.

Did I dare think God's favor was pursuing us like an unavoidable shadow?

Before we attended the Senate Higher Education Committee hearing, I was curious about the significance of Nic's death and how it related to what we were trying to accomplish. After approaching Anna, she paused and stared at me with a very compassionate and somewhat confused look.

"Greg, for years we've tried encouraging legislators to pass a meningitis vaccine law and when Jamie's situation occurred, they responded by passing the law to protect students living in a dorm. We were very appreciative, but we knew it didn't go far enough. We pushed, but they wouldn't budge. Your son's death got their attention once again and now we see a real possibility they will respond accordingly. Without Nic, we wouldn't be here."

I needed to hear that as much as I needed air to breathe. Struggling to live by Pastor Caldwell's eulogy and not get stuck on the question of "why," I always encountered it anyway just beneath my consciousness. I awoke every day with it and it followed my every thought until the weight of my fatigue crushed its pursuit and allowed me to fall asleep. My mind continued to search and search for any plausible explanation and Anna's response provided me more than a satisfactory reason.

Of course, no one could confirm my conclusion, but her answer at last brought some semblance of peace to my troubled mind. If we were successful, Nic's death would be the sole reason why the law was modified.

Arlene accompanied me again on our second trip to Austin. We drove up a day before the hearing and Anna reserved us a room in the historic Hotel Ella, a Greek revival-style mansion. Constructed in 1900, the structure is an architectural marvel with its distinctive wrap around veranda. We detected renovations made throughout the decades, but they kept the fifty-foot columns to maintain a touch of old southern charm.

Anna scheduled me an interview with one of the local television stations and because of the local traffic, we almost missed it. We hurried to check in and again, only one room was registered to us.

Really? Again? Someone had to be playing a cruel trick on us.

No big convention was in town, so I was dumbfounded why Anna booked only one room. Although Arlene and I didn't exhibit any harsh feelings towards each other, we both preferred our own rooms. Not having time to question Anna's mistake, I rushed in and freshened-up for the interview.

The meeting took place in Anna's room where she introduced me to the reporter and then named herself as my legal representative. My eyebrows shot up and my head snapped back because we never discussed it before and I wasn't sure why I needed legal representation. Was she aware of some pending litigation that involved me or was it merely a reactionary response? She had my complete confidence and if something was brewing, I trusted her to tell me.

In the days following Nic's death, I did lots of interviews, but that was one I will never forget. During most interviews, the reporters asked the same questions over and over:

"How are you holding up considering all this is taking place so soon after your son's death? And, what do you think your son would say about what you're attempting to do?"

My response became almost automatic, but not on that occasion.

The reporter said instead, "What message do you want our audience to receive from you?"

Having never been asked that question before, I paused for a second or two. Looking straight into the camera, I said, "I want them to look at me and think, *I don't want to be that guy.*"

Anna told me later my response was perfect. It was very poignant and would touch all who tuned in to see the nightly news broadcast. I was just hopeful the viewers would include members of the Higher

Education Committee.

After the interview, Anna introduced Arlene and me to Dr. Carol Baker, who was also scheduled to give testimony at the hearing. We all enjoyed a very engaging dinner, which provided an opportunity for us to learn more about vaccines and the anti-vaccine movement. We finally got around to the subject of our sleeping arrangements and Anna apologized for the oversight. She offered to get us an additional room, but we declined. Laughing, I told everyone I'll put a barricade between us to keep Arlene on her side of the bed.

The next morning, we drove a short distance to the Capital building for the much-anticipated hearing. March weather in Texas is typically pleasant, but on that particular day, the air was dense and suggested something threatening was imminent.

With no funnel clouds on the horizon nor any winter blast predicted, the real threat was hardly weather-related. The pending storm from the anti-vaxxers was gaining force and would make its arrival during the committee hearing.

With HB 1816 passed by vote out of the House's Public Health Committee, the stakes were significantly higher for the opposition. Our first win put them on notice and they had to respond more aggressively during the Senate hearing to derail whatever advantage they perceived we had obtained.

The Senate hearing room looked the same size and make-up as the House's version, except the committee was smaller, with seven members. The atmosphere was much more intense this go-round and the room was permeated with a "do or die" feel to it.

As we entered, all sorts of chatter came from the opposing groups, and this time, I found it much easier to determine friends from foes. Everyone who looked at me without a smile or friendly nod was there to oppose the bill and they numbered a lot. Many college students were in attendance and they all supported the anti-vaxxers.

TV cameras inside and outside the hearing room waited for something newsworthy to pounce on. Witnesses included experts, parents, professional organizations, college institutions, and students. Our team also anticipated the stakes to be much higher and we responded by securing a commitment from Dr. Baker to testify. As the Vice-Chair of the CDC's Advisory Committee on Immunization Practices, Dr. Baker is a nationally renowned expert on immunization. Her presence alone would outweigh the combined testimony from all supporters of the anti-vaccine community.

Senator Judith Zaffirini chaired the committee and she called the hearing to order at 9:00 on the dot. Unlike the Public Health Committee, we didn't benefit from having a senior legislator request our bill be listed first on the agenda. Because of the anticipated controversy, SB 1107 was the last bill scheduled for discussion. After hours of listening to the pros and cons of various bills—none of which we had any interest in—our time arrived.

With standing room only, people were antsy to witness the expected fireworks. Many more people who were against the bill were in attendance this time, but I couldn't determine if they all were registered to speak or not.

An overweight cameraman took his position in the east corner of the room designated for media. From that angle, he secured a perfect spot to film the speakers and the committee members.

Chairperson Zaffirini allowed the opposition to present their testimony first. Their speakers included several individuals associated with P.R.O.V.E., some parents, and a couple of students, but absent were any expert witnesses. So far, their strategy would be the same, which included unsubstantiated data and emotional testimony.

About six or seven people testified and they repeated the same ole tired message: "Vaccines contain lead, they cause autism, the government has no right to force medication against my will, it's a violation of my civil liberties, total deaths and incidents of the disease are so rare that mandatory vaccination is not necessary." One parent said he would send his daughter out of state if the law passes.

I thought, yeah right. Just wait until he sees how expensive out-of-state tuition really is and he'll have second thoughts.

They presented lots of statistics and information that seemed very questionable, but they never announced the source of their data. Students applauded the comments made by members of their party and cheered them on with verbal eruptions of "Yes!" and "That's right!"

It felt like I was attending a sports pep-rally. Their faces lit up every time they thought they scored points with the committee. Their outbursts became so distracting that the Chair instructed the students to stop. After the last person spoke, the group seemed very confident they had proved their case and thus convinced the committee to kill the bill.

Ohhhh... but then it was our turn to present our position.

Our strategy was to submit all the personal and emotional testimony first and then make a decisive point by providing all the scientific data last. As first up, I used my same speech from before except for one minor change.

The same urge that led me to write Nic's letter compelled me to add one additional statement. Before, I had questioned the urge, but now, confident God led me, my responsibility was to be obedient.

I modified my speech by adding the following: "May God help anyone who opposes this bill getting passed."

Jamie was up next and she was no less than awesome. We asked her to show her prosthetics this time to give the committee members and the opposition a first-hand view of the destruction meningitis caused in her life. During her testimony, she turned around and demonstrated her fingerless hands for all to see. She told the very students who had applauded earlier, "By not taking the vaccine, this could easily happen to you, or worse, you could die."

Very powerful!

Her sincere testimony more than made her point and moved some in the room to tears. Groans of regret were mutters by some students while others turned away to avoid looking at Jamie's disfigured hands. The once-confident smiles, flashed only minutes earlier, had changed to bowed heads of shame.

Two more mothers testified about the terrible loss of their children to the disease and the suffering they endured because of that loss. Our testimonies were so touching and empathetic that the Chair instructed the clerk to turn off the three-minute timer. The committee wanted to hear every detail of our stories and that could only be interpreted as good news for us.

Dr. Baker was up next, our star witness. Up to then, we all had done a pretty good job of "getting on base," but when Dr. Baker came up to bat, she hit a grand slam home run!

Because Dr. Baker based her outstanding testimony on convincing facts and substantial research by the medical community, she contradicted all the accusations and dispelled every statistic, rumor, and lie perpetrated by the anti-vaxxers. Her reputation as a world renowned expert and the current position she held with the CDC elevated her testimony to the highest of heights and reduced the anti-vaxxers testimony to a comical skit worthy of Saturday Night Live.

Without question, we made a quite compelling argument for the members to vote the bill out of committee. But despite the statistical and factual data Dr. Baker presented, doubts lingered whether the anti-vaxxers' threats would victimize the committee members, thus get them to kill the bill.

The decision should be a no-brainer. The science that supports vaccine safety and public health is indisputable, yet it tends to be ignored and replaced with speculation and fear when vaccine legislation is considered. Although we had scientific facts and experts backing us, the anti-vaxxers outnumbered us 10 to 1.

Like the Public Health Committee, the Senate's Higher Education Committee decided to postpone the vote for a week or two. Unlike the anti-vaxxers, I didn't presume we had the votes, but I still felt very hopeful. The assurance my faith once provided hadn't returned one hundred percent, but the gap was closing fast. After this very emotional hearing, our team gathered towards the rear of the room, and then one of the committee members approached me.

"Mr. Williams, I'm so sorry for your loss and I'm so grateful you mentioned God in your testimony. It means a lot to me."

"Thank you, Senator, I appreciate your kind words. I could never imagine testifying before a senate committee hearing, but God has led me to this point for a reason and I have to acknowledge that. Without him, I wouldn't be here."

"Indeed, Mr. Williams, and good luck to you, sir."

When he turned to leave, I had a moment to myself and I looked to the heavens and smiled. That's why God wanted me to add that statement to my speech. If those words made an impact on him, then maybe they would with the other committee members as well.

How truly amazing to witness God's work!!

Worried less about the vote's postponement, I was sure the committee's concerns were probably the same as the Public Health Committee. In time, they would vote and I expected the same outcome. Eager for resolution, I awaited the committee's decision for no other reason but to see the results of God's handiwork.

I wasn't disappointed.

About one week later, the Higher Education Committee voted 6-1 in support of the bill. I was so jubilant and in awe of God's awesomeness! Without a shadow of doubt, God's presence guided the vote of that committee. By seeing those results first hand, my faith was off the charts!!

Others might not be as convinced and would claim luck or coincidence, but I knew better. This result added up to more than chance.

God placed the right people at the right time to do the right thing, and I simply played my minor role.

Shepherding the bill through the Senate and the House Committee hearings were major accomplishments, but the next hurdle would be a much more significant challenge. The House Calendar Committee is a be-all, end-all committee that determines what bills will be discussed on the House floor. This is where a lot of well-intentioned bills die either through a lack of support, a lack of time, or a political quid pro quo.

If our bill was not scheduled by the Calendar Committee, we were done. *Go ahead and stick a fork in us.*

With around 40 days remaining in the session, we didn't trust our bills would work their way through the process by themselves. Anna was very worried the bills would die while waiting to get on the legislative calendar. She proposed a strategy to contact all Calendar Committee members and encourage them to include our bill on their legislative agenda.

Anna, Patsy, and I attempted to scheduled appointments with the committee members. When we made those calls, the first question the staffer always asked was, "Are you a member of the legislator's district?" If so, our chances of seeing a legislator up close and personal were much greater.

We pleaded our case, hoping to make a positive impression with the staffers. In our desperate mode, someone was better than no one. Through one of the conversations, I discovered the anti-vaxxers were making the same calls, but of course, with a very contrasting plea.

Of the members we contacted, only one agreed to meet with us, Rep. Garnet Coleman of Houston. We met at his office and five minutes into the conversation I wanted to shout to the rooftops, "Hallelujah and Thank You, Jesus!!!"

While attempting to gain his support, we discovered one of his best friends died from bacterial meningitis years earlier. He assured us the bill would be included on the Calendar and sent to the House floor for a vote.

Again, the manifestation of God's blessings and grace seemed to answer every obstacle we faced. A total reversal of my hospital experience, God's presence was unquestionable.

First, I encountered Rep. Howard, who had lost a son, and then Rep. Coleman, who lost a best friend to meningitis. Both men identified with my loss and purpose. No one on earth could have predicted this connection and I cannot deny that God's love for me was the reason they were in a position to help us.

I shouldn't have been surprised by Rep. Coleman's assurance, but seeing God's grace again and again was something for which I had no point of reference. If my faith was off the charts before, it was now limitless. *God's love is just mindboggling!*

Like Rep. Howard, Rep. Coleman was true to his word. The Calendar Committee scheduled May 6th as the date the House would vote on the bill. I debated whether or not to attend.

With so much riding on the vote, the pressure would be too intense watching it live. If we failed, it would feel like losing Nic all over again and I could not expose myself to that agony.

But, on the other hand, to be there in person and observe the interactions of the full legislature would be an incredible experience. After working so hard politicking and giving heart-wrenching testimony, I would have been irresponsible not to attend.

Arlene decided against it and I understood her reasoning. Patsy joined me and planned to stay all day if necessary. She lived in Austin, so no travel concerns on her part. We met and took our seats in the gallery, hoping our bill would be at the top of the agenda.

No such luck.

We waited and watched the ongoing discussions of legislators in favor of and in opposition to bill after bill after bill. Unless you were there to support a specific piece of legislation, changing a flat was more exciting.

At last, I received a text from one of Rep. Howard's staffers that we were up next. As well dressed as a GQ model, Rep. Howard approached the podium and the pulsating rhythm of my heart throbbed with anticipation. Even though aware of divine intervention permeating our every move, I still felt antsy we wouldn't get all the votes needed.

As Rep. Howard addressed the legislators, I wanted to scream at them to shut up and listen so they could understand why passing the bill was so important. How soon I forgot my own recent attitude. Our bill was as pointless to others as their bill was to us. Legislators don't hesitate to hold their sidebar conversations, working on their laptops and not paying much attention to Rep. Howard. I was going nuts sitting on the edge of my seat, confused by the nonchalant attitude of his fellow legislators. Of course, the vote meant the world to me, but like the bills before mine, no one had much interest aside from Patsy and me.

Rep. Howard completed his talk in support of the bill and then it was time to take a vote.

With my eyes closed and head bowed, I whispered a quick prayer. "God, please lead these legislators to vote in favor of the bill. It will undoubtedly save lives and create a lasting legacy for Nic. In Jesus name, I pray. Amen."

Witnessing the minor miracles first hand, my confidence should have been firmly in gear, but my experience with Nic had taught me to be guarded about expectations, be they realistic or impractical.

If anyone understood my emotions at that moment, Patsy did. She was in the same position back in 2009 when the 81st Legislature passed the original meningitis bill.

With a hint of uncertainty in my voice, I said to her, "So, what do you think? Will they pass it?"

Without blinking an eye, she responded with an air of absolute confidence. "Hell, yeah, Greg! We got this."

Very hopeful, of course, but Patsy's assurance eluded me. I could never forget how assured I had been of Nic's transfer and how hopeless I had felt after it was denied.

We turned our attention back to the House floor and watched the legislators cast their votes. The galley is the second level of an arena-type room with the center open for observation of the first floor. The tiered seats circled the room and provided a clear view looking down at the legislators. Their oak wooden desks resembled a 19th-century style with the writing surface able to be opened for storage. The burgundy high-back leather chairs were of the same era and adorned with the State of Texas seal on their backs. While still carrying on their conversations, they cast votes electronically from their desk.

One by one, the lights from the tabulation board lit up by the name of each legislator. Some red lights indicated a nay vote, but the greens lights outnumbered them by far.

After a few minutes, the tabulation was complete. It wasn't unanimous, but I considered it a landslide! The House voted 122 - 14 in favor of HB 1816.

Thank You, God!!

Patsy shouted, "See, I told ya!!" She gave me a high five and we embraced with a hug filled with rejoice and relief.

"I can't believe it. We actually did it."

"Yes, we did, and Nic is so proud of you."

For the first time in weeks, I felt the joy that represents God's love.

The passage of the House bill was truly a miracle and I was so appreciative for everyone who assisted us. Now the Senate needed to pass their version of it as well. Because Senate Bill 1107 was a companion bill, it was a foregone conclusion that passage by the Senate would be all but automatic.

On May 11th, just five days after the House voted, the Senate was scheduled to vote on SB1107. Because of job obligations, I couldn't attend the session, but Patsy assured me she would be there with "bells on." She also promised to call me right away after the Senate took their vote.

Knowing it could take all day before they voted, I tried with no success to keep busy. Every time my phone rang, I expected it to be Patsy. After each call, my expectation grew exponentially, hoping the next one would be Patsy.

The anticipation and pressure escalated to a point that I made myself sick. My not taking a break and not going to lunch made the waiting almost unbearable. Constantly looking at my watch didn't make the time go by quicker and starving myself made matters worse.

Finally, around 2:30, Patsy called. The Senate voted 29-2 in support of the bill!

We claimed another miracle! I hadn't been that excited since the day of Nic's birth.

Tears of joy streamed from my emotion-filled

eyes. I called Arlene and emailed everyone of the unimaginable news!! Both chambers had approved their respective bills with at least ninety percent of the legislators voting yes.

Highly improbable, but with God, all things are possible.

We had come so far so fast and, although a novice with the whole legislative process, I knew deep inside me that what we achieved to that point was not the norm.

Every accomplishment and every vote was undeniably attributed to God's intervention. In all my years of being a Christian, I never observed or was involved with anything or anyone where God's will was as evident as his parting of the Red Sea. Although not hearing God speak audibly or see a clear vision in a dream, I sensed his presence leading us every step of the way.

The votes were yet another incredible victory, but we couldn't afford to celebrate very long. The final and most difficult obstacle was convincing Governor Perry to sign the bill into law. We had a genuine concern he would veto the bill because of his involvement with the whole HPV fiasco. We were told by a very credible source that the anti-vaxxers had scheduled an appointment with Gov. Perry, so we were determined to get equal time.

After brainstorming a list of people who may have some influence with the governor, Ms. Dodie came to mind. After the funeral, she had asked me to sit with her during a Lakewood Service. I accommodated her request and she introduced me to the congregation and shared Nic's story. When the service ended, she mentioned that if I ever needed anything to contact her.

At that time, her offer didn't register with me, but that all changed with the passage of the bill. After contacting one of Ms. Dodie's assistants, we were told that Gov. Perry knows the Osteen family well and she may be in a position to help us.

Confident we had obtained the magic touch, I thought anything we attempted would be like taking candy from a baby. Boy, was I wrong!!!

I discovered it to be a bit challenging even contacting Ms. Dodie. After reviewing my phone records, I determined the call I had received from her was an unlisted number. I phoned the church, hoping to schedule an appointment, but the protocol dictated for a letter to be written and delivered to the receptionist, and then Ms. Dodie would read it.

I complied with the instructions and within my letter's content, I asked if she could contact Gov. Perry and request a meeting on our behalf.

Impatient while waiting a couple of days, I received her call. Before she even greeted me, I was prepared to interrupt her and get straight to the point of asking what day were we meeting with Gov. Perry. With so many things falling perfectly in place, my confidence assured me the meeting was already scheduled!

Needless to say, I was disappointed, but not deterred, when she mentioned that getting us in to meet with the Governor was beyond her capabilities. She was very supportive and encouraging of our efforts, but she couldn't help us.

Due to our recent successes, I'll now admit I had become presumptuous, but this setback served to confirm I had to keep working my butt off to get the bill signed into law. It's good to have faith, but as I wrote earlier, "faith without works is dead."

I pressed on.

As each day passed, my desperation escalated with fear of not having an opportunity to make our case. The Senate passed the bill on May 11th, and the session would end on May 30th. We had 21 days remaining and we were still as close to meeting Gov. Perry as we might have been with meeting President Obama.

Surely, God would not have brought us that far and then abandon us.

At one point, I was tempted to camp outside the Governor's mansion until someone felt enough sympathy for me to schedule that elusive, but all important, appointment.

My buddy, Stud, maintained multiple connections to the Gov. Perry, but they all failed to materialize. The legislative time clock kept ticking and I was helpless to stop it.

Feeling like a caged animal desperate to free itself, I perceived the steel bars of access to Gov.

Perry solidify my confinement. Without much more to do but wait it out, I hoped for the best.

My desperation didn't yield any results but that was hardly a reason to be discouraged. Not at that moment. Not after seeing firsthand the will of God. I was confident Gov. Perry would sign the bill whether we met with him or not.

The scenario took me back three months earlier while spending every waking moment praying for God's intervention. Then, I couldn't find much evidence to suggest God was even listening. Certainly he was, but he allowed other plans to take their course. My desired outcome for Nic didn't happen then, but this time, I felt thankful to have God's full involvement.

With about seven days remaining before the session ended, I received a phone call from Floyd LeBlanc. An executive with Centerpoint Energy, Floyd informed me that one of their lobbyists was meeting with Gov. Perry soon regarding a pending business deal and he would ask the lobbyist to find out if the Governor would meet with us.

About that same time, the Texas Medical Association (TMA) contacted me to assist with an op-ed article to encourage Gov. Perry to sign the meningitis bill. TMA was formed in 1853 and is the nation's largest and most powerful state medical association. Representing thousands of physicians throughout the state, their sole purpose is improving health for all Texans.

I jumped at the opportunity. If we couldn't meet with the Governor personally, an op-ed from such a respected organization provided us a small window of opportunity to get our message through. Patsy and Dr. Baker joined my efforts and we provided the association several quotes for the article.

On May 25th, TMA distributed a news release entitled, "Doctors Urge Governor Perry to Sign Meningitis Bill."

With only five days remaining in the session, their timing was perfect. The piece included all our quotes and made a very convincing case that the law would save lives and prevent unnecessary hardships for victims of meningitis. We hoped the article, coming from such an esteemed and professional organization, would encourage the governor to sign the bill. But still, we didn't have any clue of his intentions.

Waiting to hear from Floyd was almost as stressful as waiting on that dreaded transfer call. Finally, on May 26th, he called. Anita Perry, the Governor's wife, was a former nurse and rumor had it that she supported the bill one hundred percent. Floyd ended the call by saying that Gov. Perry would sign it into law.

All our hopes and prayers were answered. At that point, we had no need to meet with the Governor. Because of God's unconditional love, the impossible would soon become a blessed reality.

On May 27, 2011, Governor Perry signed into law the Jamie Schanbaum & Nicolis Williams Act.

Around 7:00 p.m. I received the call at my home. My immediate reaction was a sense of extreme accomplishment mixed with profound relief. To go from not even knowing who represented me in the Texas Legislature to getting a bill signed into law was nothing short of a miracle.

I gave God all the credit and praise. Without his love, grace, and mercy, nothing we accomplished would have been possible. Absolutely nothing.

Because of the law, countless lives will be spared and, to boot, Nic has a legacy established in his name. Nothing I will do for the remainder of my life will give me more pleasure than what we accomplished. The following scripture couldn't be more fitting:

You intended to harm me, but God intended it for good to accomplish what is now being done, the saving of lives.

Genesis 50:20

CHAPTER 14

SO

Being a parent for half my life, I'm convinced there is no gift greater than being blessed with a child. For many, the love of a parent for their child is limitless and unconditional. It demonstrates a depth of compassion and a lifelong commitment unmatched by any other relationship.

Without hesitation or fear, some parents will do almost anything to protect the lives of their children. In fact, many would give their life to save the life of their child. Such a sacrifice is the ultimate gauge in measuring the love of a parent.

However, that sacrifice falls short to a great degree in comparison to God's love for humanity. The characterization of his love is measured by the most eloquent and consequential scripture in the bible.

For God so loved the world that he gave his one and only Son, that whoever believes in him shall not perish but have eternal life.

John 3:16 NIV

For a word that consists of only two letters, "So" is monumental in capturing the maximum of whatever one is describing. God's love of mankind is "So" abundant that he gave his son to die for us.

Before reading any further, take a second to just think about "so" and how powerfully it conveys God's love. We love our children enough to die for them, but how many parents would ask their child to die for someone else?

The extreme of that "so" is inconceivable to humanity, yet it describes with complete accuracy the depth of God's love. I'm not aware of anyone I love "so" to a point I would allow my child to die for them. I'm confident no parent anywhere would be willing to request that of their child.

Moreover, how many of us love our parents "so" that we would be willing to die, and die a horrific death out of love and obedience? Not many, if any one at all. Jesus knew his fate well in advance and because of the "so" of his love for God, he was willing to obey and give his life in an unimaginable and horrific manner.

With that much abundance of love and sacrifice, how could anyone dare to ask God anything, let alone 'why' concerning our own selfish issues?

Maybe before posing that 'why' question, we should instead ask, "Why do you love me so?"

Like our biological parents, God wants the very best for us. After all, he created us in his own image and what parent doesn't feel a sense of pride and satisfaction at seeing their child succeed and become all they are destined to be? As an added gift, he desires to give us everlasting life in heaven.

In return, all he asks is a belief and trust in his son, Jesus Christ.

Because of humanity's shortcomings and God's "so" love, Jesus was sent to demonstrate God's purpose for our lives. Jesus' life and time with mankind represented three simple lessons to live by: to love, to serve, and to teach.

When applying those principals, life's meaning becomes clear. The principals won't prevent tragedies or storms from affecting your life, but they do prepare and guide you through the process. When a storm does arrive, faith must be unwavering; love, unconditional; and obedience, unquestionable.

As the storm of my life cleared, the pending sunshine provided ample points of reflection.

Thrilled at receiving the news of the bill's passage, I was also relieved that the journey had reached its destination. For weeks, my every waking moment was focused on nothing else besides getting the bill passed. A heavy burden was lifted, but I believed the news would, as if by magic, heal my broken heart and bring me peace of mind.

To my sad surprise, it did not. It helped in many ways, but the realization of knowing that nothing would ever fill the void of Nic's death became more apparent to me.

Several months after the bill was signed into

law, my struggle continued, caused by not having an opportunity to say goodbye to Nic in a way that I desired. I found some peace with my letter of love and admiration for him; however, he didn't have an opportunity to reciprocate that message. Although many of his friends talked with me after the funeral and described how much he cared for his family, it just wasn't the same as hearing from him.

One day out of the blue, Arlene called to tell me about a letter she found. Nic wrote it about three years earlier and she suggested I come by to read it. He had addressed it to both of us:

"I sincerely appreciate you for everything you have ever done for me. You raised me in a loving home and provided everything I could ever need in my life. You have always forgiven me even though I gave you plenty of reasons not to. Whatever activity I attempted, you always supported me even when I didn't do my best. Lastly and more importantly, I know you love me. In return, I want you to know I love you too. Your son, Nicolis Williams"

His brief letter released the intolerable sorrow I carried and reminded me of a very popular song from 1974. *Cats in the Cradle* by Harry Chapin was about a father who is too busy to spend time with his son. Though the son asks him to join in childhood activities, the father always responds with little more than vague promises of spending time together in the 'future.' While wishing to spend time with his father, the son starts to model himself on his father's behavior, hence the verse wishing to be "just like him."

The final two verses are a reverse of the roles, where the father asks his grown-up son to visit, but the son responds that he is now too busy to find the time for his father. The father then reflects that they are both alike.

Growing up in the 70's, I listened to Motown artists such as Stevie Wonder, Marvin Gaye, and the Jackson 5, so I never understood why that song resonated with me. In hindsight, I believe God was preparing me even as a teenager for the role I was to play in my children's lives. I was determined to be the complete opposite of the dad in the song.

Without a shadow of doubt, I identified with how Nic must have felt after reading my letter. Neither of us knew it at the time, but our letters could be interpreted as our goodbyes to each other. His letter brought me back full circle to the song I heard all those years ago. The last verse in the song reads "And as I hung up the phone, it occurred to me--- He'd grown up just like me. My boy was just like me."

I will never understand the purpose of my son's death. But I cannot deny God's influence on how he more than prepared me prior to Nic's death and how his love guided me afterwards. The following are just some of the remarkable events that occurred and the people who were placed in strategic positions to be utilized by God in revealing his purpose, his presence, and his love:

1) My father provided an excellent example of a role model for me. I learned the value of commitment and responsibility, and about the special bond between a father and his children. Through his parental love, I developed the most significant characteristic of being a man and one of which I'm most proud: a loving father.

2) Months before Nic's death, the urge to write the goodbye letter was unavoidable. As much as I tried to ignore the urge, it pursued me until I conceded. It brought me much needed comfort to know Nic knew how much he was loved.

3) The relationships with Trish and Sarah helped prepare me for the role and direction I took after Nic's death. Someone once said that people enter into our lives for a reason or a season and this was so true of these two special women. They are not involved in my life at the writing of this book, but when they were, they provided the clarity I needed to pursue the path I took. They more than served the purpose God intended for them. To confirm my belief that Sarah's prediction was meant for my son Nico, I contacted her to see if she continued having those feelings of her son's pending death. I was not surprised when she told me the feelings stopped after Nic died.

4) On Feb. 9th, our second day in College Station, the temperature dropped below freezing and we didn't have any winter clothes. When I departed the hospital to buy some clothes, a bitter cold slapped me with such velocity that it almost turned me back. Someone noticed how underdressed I was and offered me their heavy leather jacket to battle the elements outside.

With so much going on that day, I didn't remember who gave me their jacket. Several days later, I contacted my brother-in-law, David, and thanked him for the gesture. He said it wasn't his jacket and he didn't recognize it.

I was puzzled as to whom it belonged. The coat was quite expensive and very well manufactured, not one easily discarded. I called Gabby and asked her to inquire about it with Nic's friends, but she drew a blank as well. I called Nic's roommates and they were just as clueless.

Weeks passed and no one contacted me about returning the jacket or responded to my inquiries. Till this day, its true owner remains a mystery. Was an angel among us that cold and dreadful day?

5) While in route back to Houston after cleaning Nic's room, the radiator of Arlene's friend's van ran hot. As we exited the van, the radiator leaked a steady flow of antifreeze. It was seriously low of water and we were several exits from the nearest gas station.

Given the situation, we had no way to keep our appointment with the church scheduled for 2:00 that day. The appointment was the first meeting to plan Nic's funeral, so it was critical we kept it.

Arlene suggested a bottle of water might do the trick. One of Nic's roommates had provided her a bottle of water before we left and she was naïve to believe it would be enough to get us to the nearest gas station. With an obvious leak in the radiator, any water would pour right through it.

Her friend said, "Why not? It's better than walking." He poured the water into the radiator and it didn't leak out!!

I didn't believe it would last, but we went with it. He started up the van and puttered along for about a mile-and-a-half before we reached a gas station. There, he filled the radiator to the brim, but still it leaked and at some point we would be in the same position all over again.

We were not going to keep our appointment so I asked Arlene to call and cancel. Her friend was insistent that we would make it back to Houston in time for the meeting.

But how? There was no way! If the van ran out of water once and we didn't do anything to repair the leak, the radiator would drain again. He had faith that the van would make it and sure enough, it did.

6) During the repast meal, I felt the absolute worst at any time up to that particular point. After

sitting through the funeral and watching the hearse carry Nic's body away to an incinerator, I had all I could take and on the very edge of losing it.

Then one by one, Nic's friends approached to tell me how much he loved me. I felt like they were in line waiting to offer words of encouragement and to acknowledge Nic's feelings for me. Their brief stories saved me that horrible day and also provided me the strength to press forward. Their timing was divinely perfect.

7) A short while after the bill was signed into law, I was driving to work when all of a sudden a gargantuan rush of emotion overcame me. It was so overwhelming and unexpected that I exited the freeway as soon as I could.

With all that had occurred the past few months, I thought, *Now what, a heart attack?*

It wasn't. I couldn't then—and I doubt I will ever—find accurate words to describe the intensity of what I felt. The feeling's origin was of love, but it was a love magnified a thousand-fold. I felt as if God had embraced me and affirmed my efforts for being obedient.

My heart wasn't racing but the magnitude of compassion, love, and warmth were all-consuming. It was pure unadulterated love in its truest form. I never felt that before or since, but I was comforted to know God was pleased with my efforts. Now, I can claim to have the personal relationship with God that I longed for!

8) Rep. Charlie was a man of faith first and foremost, but he was also recognized as the most conservative member of the Texas House. So much so, in 2011 he was named "The Most Famously Red Member of the Texas House." To take on our cause went against everything his party stood for, yet he used all his political weight to clear a way to victory.

9) Three years after Nic died, I received an email alerting me about Kyle Schmidt, another Texas A&M student who contracted bacterial meningitis. Before I contacted the family, I found his amazing story on Facebook and got a quick update. He took the meningitis vaccine as required by law, but he still contracted the disease.

There are five strains of the disease, but vaccines were available for only four at that time. Kyle's doctors at the hospital concluded he contracted the one strain without a vaccine and they treated him with antibiotics. A devout Christian family, they requested prayers on his behalf. It was "touch and go" for a while but, he survived the attack.

I had an opportunity to talk with Kyle's mother, Barbie Schmidt, and she thanked me for doing all we did to get the law modified. She believed our efforts saved her son's life. According to her son's doctor, Kyle would have died had he not taken the vaccine when entering college. Although the vaccine wasn't for the particular strain of meningitis he contracted, doctors believed it slowed the disease's progression enough to enable them to treat him with success.

At the conclusion of our conversation, I was reminded of the brief talk by Pastor Walker during Nic's service. He posed the question, "How does this fit all things?"

Now we know.

During my time in the Texas legislature, I repeated the same message many times: "The law will save lives, but unfortunately; we will never know who those students will be and the impact they will have on our society."

I never imagined talking with a family member whose child in fact benefited from the law. It gave me an incredible feeling to know our efforts helped save a life. It was worth everything we fought so hard to accomplish. All the tears, the insecurities, the politicking, the emotional testimonies, the worries, the anger, the heartache, the sleepless nights, the frustration, and the struggles were all worth the effort in saving that student's life and for those to come.

No matter what we encounter during our brief time on this earth, we should always praise God, regardless of the circumstance. It's certainly a lot easier to do when things are going great, but the same adulation—or even more—should be given when heartache and trouble arrive.

Abandoning God, or even questioning his existence, is not difficult when our needs are not met or our prayers go unanswered. Many times we perceive God's inaction as an inconsistency, and inconsistency creates doubt, which ultimately leads to a loss of faith or disbelief in God altogether.

During these very times, our love and trust for God must be resilient and unconditional to contest the temptation of doubt. It's human nature to forget the good times or blessings in our lives and quite easy to remember the times when things didn't go our way. We will face significant difficulties and challenges throughout our lives and how we respond is a direct reflection of our faith in our Lord and Savior, Jesus Christ.

I started my journey as a faithful Christian, but one without encountering my own personal storm. At the storm's conclusion, my faith had grown to unimaginable heights by experiencing first hand God's ability to do anything and by witnessing his unconditional love.

He opened doors that I had perceived were slammed shut. I watched with amazement as he changed the hearts and minds of people who opposed us. He made a way when there was no way.

My obedience and willingness formed the foundation that allowed God to use me. His response to my "why" was the impetus for all the extraordinary events and also to bring me the people who all seemed to serve a particular purpose in helping me complete my journey.

You have a purpose as well and it's up to you to see through the distractions and recognize God's answer to your "Why?" You may find it perfectly acceptable and enlightening to ask God why, but you must be prepared and willing to take on his response.

Even as Jesus was dying on the cross, he asked God why.

About three in the afternoon, Jesus cried out in a loud voice, "My God, my God, why have you forsaken me?"
Matthew 27:46

My own response wasn't immediate, but in gradual steps God presented a purpose for me regarding Nic's death. That purpose could only be revealed if my mind was receptive and I was willing to be obedient. Had I gotten stuck on my anger or disappointment with God, I would have missed the opportunity to fulfill his purpose.

God's will hadn't caused Nic's death, but he did allow it to happen. The story could have ended there, but my pursuit of "why" allowed me to see a more fulfilling picture.

As you encounter trials of life, remain steadfast in faith, push past the 'dissats,' and ask God how you can use the situation to grow his kingdom. Your willingness and obedience to God's response will determine your journey.

APPENDIX

A LIFE LETTER TO MY SON

I'm writing you this letter for two reasons:

(1) because I love you with all my heart, and

(2) to give you something tangible to remember me after I depart to the tennis courts in heaven.

Don't get me wrong, I am planning on being here for quite some time, but the purpose of these pages is to give you support and guidance when I am no longer around to speak with you in person. I decided to write this in longhand because it should have more meaning to you and also because I hope you can hear my voice as you read these pages. This is my attempt to share with you some encouraging words and the benefits of some of my experiences that occurred during my time on this earth.

Before he died, my dad left me a half-dollar coin with my name scratched on it and I cherish that coin. I hope you will feel the same way about this letter.

As the years pass by and you read this letter again and again, I hope it brings you comfort and joy knowing that you are the best son I could ever imagine and that I love you unconditionally.

First, I want to apologize for disrupting your life because of the divorce. You and Tiffany were innocent victims of my inability to correct the problems of my failing marriage and I am deeply remorseful for the pain I caused you. I made mistakes and did things I am not proud of, but the one great accomplishment that I most appreciate and that also brought me years of profound pleasure is the birth of my one and only son!!

As a little boy, and later as you grew older, you always had difficulty being accepted by your peers. I am not sure if this will continue throughout your life, but I hope it doesn't. As a child, I always needed attention and affirmation and when I became an adult, that need still resided deep within my genetic footprint.

My advice is to do some soul searching and determine where your need to be accepted originated. Before you discover the origin, first acknowledge if that need truly exists. Acceptance of a problem is the first step in overcoming it. Most people cannot look into the mirror and see any character flaws in their reflection.

We all have them, so never question yourself about why you are the only one. *You're not.*

It's even okay and I highly recommend you speak with a therapist regarding any problem you deem too overwhelming. I did it several times during my marriage with your mother, which brought me lots of clarity and a different perspective on many of the issues I faced during the most difficult time of my life.

All people are flawed to a degree and they may accept you or reject you for whatever reason they determine. The thing to remember is that you are not perfect, but you are a kind, thoughtful, and considerate young man who sincerely appreciates their companionship. When exhibiting those characteristics and they reject you, it's their loss.

Always treat people honestly and with respect, and the rest will take care of itself. When you practice this concept, you can look in the mirror and know it was not you who failed the relationship.

Being a man in this complicated world has lots of interpretations and societal expectations. Make it your decision to define what you desire your manhood to be and never allow someone else's expectations to dictate your definition. Trust me, I wish I had learned that lesson years ago.

I could write what I believe are the appropriate characteristics of a man, but my definitions would be a reflection of my own experiences and expectations. More important is for you to decide early on which characteristics will define your manhood and incorporate them into your consciousness. They should be your core values and they do not change with the times or with the people who enter and exit your life. They should remain constant and they will guide your actions, character, behavior, and thought processes.

I will share with you just one characteristic by which I have lived my life, the one of which I am most proud. I chose to be a responsible, participative, and loving father. For me, that was my Number One priority of manhood, and the commitment has enriched my life beyond measure. There are just so many negative statistics about children growing up in a home without a father and the numbers get much worse with African-American families.

So, when I decided to have you and Tiffany, I would not entertain any question about my commitment and dedication to you. I could fail at any and everything else in my life, but I knew I would always be there for you.

"Be there" means more than providing the necessities of life. My father loved me dearly, but his generation believed if you provided food, shelter, and clothing—"the necessities"—then you were considered a good father. I desired to go much further than provide the necessities, so I was "THERE" and loved every second of it.

Whatever you decide your characteristics to be,

stay committed and do not waiver.

I hope you are fortunate enough to get married one day. Marriage is probably the most difficult adjustment you will make in your life but, if you choose the right woman, your life will be enhanced beyond your wildest imagination.

So, how do you go about picking a wife?

First, you have to know yourself through and through, including all aspects of your personality. Knowing your likes and dislikes is not enough. You have to dig much deeper and discover answers to the 'whys.'

'Why does this anger you?' or 'Why do you want this and reject that?' are the types of questions that delve deep into your psyche and reveal who you really are. I strongly encourage you and your prospective mate to read the book, *The Five Love Languages*, and I promise it will provide profound insight on how you need to be loved and how to love her in return.

Most men are very visual, so it would not surprise me if you fell for someone who's a real beauty. It is very common with men to rate physical beauty as a prerequisite in choosing a wife and that's fine, as long as it's not the only reason. Beauty will fade with time, but good character traits will last a lifetime.

Like your self-evaluation, you have to try to understand who she is and how she came to be that person. The best way to receive answers is by getting to know her family. Observe and observe even more! See how they interact, handle adversity, and handle money. More than anything else, pay very close attention to how her mother responds and interacts with her father. Of course it's not one hundred percent guaranteed, but more than likely, she will treat you in the same manner.

If you see something in her personality that just does not seem right with you, DONT IGNORE IT! That's your inner voice of reason battling your emotions and trying to get your attention. Whatever that "something" may be, it will definitely get worse as time passes. Please do not fool yourself and make the common mistake of believing she will change or that you can live with "it." SHE WILL NOT CHANGE and NEITHER WILL YOU.

I still believe in my theory of the 4 C's that attribute to a complete and successful marriage. If you recall, they are Compatibility, Communication, Compromise, and Christ.

I consider the 4 C's the foundation on which to build a happy and fulfilling marriage. They are equally significant and all should be present in the woman you choose to be your life partner.

Other than Christ, Communication is my favorite of the 4 C's. If you have good communication skills, you can overcome almost any obstacle. You have to know her inside and out to navigate the challenges with effective communication. You have to humble yourself and really see things from her perspective.

The most valuable component of communication is the ability to listen. Try repeating to her the statement she made to you. This exercise demonstrates you are listening and her intended message was received.

When everything else fails, always attempt to communicate. It will save your marriage!

She should be your queen, so always treat her with respect and honor even when you happen to be upset with her. Never start something with her that you do not intend to maintain and always put her first above everybody else.

The following is my brief advice on the all-important subject of sex... It is none of my business to know your sexual preferences, so I'm going on assumption here. Lots of men enjoy watching pornos and, if you do, don't buy into the perceived reality of what you see. All that crap is just acting and most women don't want any part of that in a genuine loving relationship.

You can discover what she desires and what pleases her by trial and error. Or do not be embarrassed to ask her what she likes. You never know unless you ask and it could significantly reduce any unmet expectations on her part. Never expect her to do anything that is painful or disrespectful to her. Lastly, remember the goal should always be mutual pleasure and respect.

Also, do not buy into the marketing hype regarding the American Dream, which is a bunch of BS, and you should avoid the temptation at all costs! The American Dream is all about uncontrollable debt that suggests the ideology of "you deserve it and you deserve it now!"

Everybody wants a new car, a big house, extravagant vacations, name brand clothes, and the list goes on and on... A simple financial rule to live by is this: "If you cannot afford it, then you do not need it."

That statement is a lot easier said than to live by, but it becomes a little easier when you make the commitment to live by what your income allows. Besides a house and car, your complete budget should also include allocations for savings, investments, tithes, emergencies, entertainment, vacations, college funds, and even Christmas gifts.

Do not buy a house that costs two times more than your combined annual income. It may be the largest purchase you make during your lifetime, but try to buy a house that is comfortable enough to live in for life.

As their income increases over time, many people will upgrade two or three houses during their lives. I dislike this strategy because you start from scratch for each new house purchase and you never get a jump on things. If you keep the same house and your income increases over time, you will have more funds to invest and retire early.

Any increase in salary should always go to your investments. Set up a budget and allocate for everything. Stick to it, no matter how difficult it may be, and it will pay big dividends in the long run. A budget is simply a plan or financial road map to help guide you through life. Always remember: *If you do* not have a plan, you are planning to fail.

If you have to buy a new car, buy it used after one or two years. A new car depreciates ten percent the moment you drive it out of the dealership's lot. So you are just throwing your hard earned money out the window as you drive off. Not very smart!!

Money can be a huge problem within a marriage and it drives many to divorce court. To help guarantee you do not take a similar trip, make sure you are both on the same financial page. And, do not wait until you are married to explore her views on finances.

Remember, communication is the key! Plan out your financial future together and keep in mind, plans need to be flexible enough to accommodate unexpected expenditures. Decide early on how many children you both want and the years apart you want them.

Tip: having two in college at the same time will cost you considerably, so plan ahead.

Plan and take vacations. You and your family deserve it and you will cherish the memories forever. Above everything else, do not play the game of "Keeping up with the Joneses." It is okay to live at a frugal level, but you must put forth the effort to find time to enjoy life. Doing fun things with your family does not have to cost an arm and a leg. A great family vacation to Europe would be a wonderful experience, but it will be very expensive.

Some of the most memorable moments of my

life were with you and Tiffany doing simple things like flying a kite or having a picnic at the park. The amount of money spent on a vacation does not determine the amount of joy, fun, and excitement, but quality time together does.

I hope you are blessed with having children one day and I hope they are spitting images of you! Be prepared for the time commitment children demand and deserve.

I recommend spending several years with your wife before the little monsters come along. For when they do, everything will change and your life as you knew it will never be the same.

If you are not ready to put in the time, then postpone having children for a while. When the monsters arrive, you will notice an immediate change in your relationship with your wife. There is a bond between a mother and child that you cannot penetrate. Just accept it and help out from day one when the baby comes home and keep helping throughout their lives.

Your wife will appreciate it and your lives together will be far less challenging. It helps build a foundation of support and trust that will be thoroughly tested while raising the children.

As a mother, your wife will more than likely take on the brunt of the child raising responsibilities. Society suggests this is her traditional role, but if you buy into that tradition and don't assist her, your marriage will suffer and you can forget about having a sex life! Your marriage will become a shell of what it was before children, which opens the door to marital dissatisfaction. If you desire to maintain what you had before, then help her with the child rearing responsibilities and your efforts will be rewarded and done so quite abundantly!

Kids are tons of fun when they are infants and toddlers, so enjoy every moment of it because the time goes by so fast. When they become teenagers, your sanity will be routinely tested and I recommend you and your wife develop an effective plan when dealing with the problems of that age.

Always present to them as one unit with the same message. They learn very early that if they split you two up, their chances of success are much greater. You may disagree behind closed doors, but always support each other in front of the monsters.

Remember, yelling or screaming does not prove a point. Use logic in your argument and keep in mind, this is just another stage they are going through. We all did, as did you, so do not be too hard on them. Try to remember when you were that age and you didn't have the knowledge you do now. If your memory serves you well, you just may be able to see their point of view.

I am not suggesting by acknowledging their point of view that you give in to their demands. Seeing their point of view allows you to empathize with them, but due to your experience and maturity, your conclusion will be much different.

Do not be too harsh when issuing punishments

for inappropriate behavior. Your punishment should be a lesson-learning opportunity and make a point, but it should not scar your child for life. They will not be perfect, so learn to forgive and to do it right away. Tell them you love them often, especially if you have a son.

Many sons and fathers sometimes experience difficulty expressing themselves to each other, which has the potential to create lifelong problems for each. It is perfectly normal and I highly recommend having an open loving relationship with your son the same way you do with your daughter. I do with you and I have relished an absolute joy in a close relationship with my best friend.

Even when money is not an issue, do not buy them everything they want. It will be very difficult not to give in to the peer pressure of "keeping up with the Joneses," but stick by your commitment. To prevent a sense of entitlement, make your children earn some of the things they desire. As they mature throughout their lives, they will learn to appreciate your efforts in developing their independence.

As parents, it is not your sole responsibility to support your children through their college career. Of course, you should help out where you can, but it is not your total financial responsibility. Again, they will appreciate it more if they earn it. It is their future and hence, they should invest in it by working as they go through or by taking out a reasonable loan.

Get into a good church and participate in one or more of its ministries. Study the bible and live by God's word. I know… that sounds funny coming from me. As they say, "better late than never." I made lots of mistakes doing what I believed what was best for me, but had I understood the blueprint for my life, I might not be divorced today, plus I would have been much happier years ago.

Life is going to throw you lots of obstacles, temptations, and sorrow, but if you really seek God's words and live by them, the meaning of your life will make sense to you and will be so much more enjoyable.

My favorite scripture in the bible is Proverbs 3:5-6. It speaks about always acknowledging God first and he will guide your path. Hindsight is always 20-20, but I am thankful God allowed me to live long enough to see what is important in life.

There will be times in your life when you will want to just give up and quit. Don't! This is the very moment when Satan will tempt you the most. You may feel vulnerable and you may believe there is no way out, but that's when your faith is all you have and your belief in God will see you through your troubles. He will, and he promises that he will.

There is nothing in life more comforting than knowing God keeps his promises.

Learn to enjoy life and take time to smell the roses or dance in the rain. Find one or two activities that truly bring you lots of joy. It does not have to be anything competitive, but it should be an activity that brings you peace of mind.

And it's a good idea to find one or two activities that you and your wife enjoy together. This helps in establishing that solid foundation of marriage I wrote about earlier. Try to find joy and peace in some of God's greatest creations.

For me, the beauty of the clear blue sea is majestic and magical, and it demonstrates God's love. I never tire of listening to wave after wave crash into the shoreline. It's beautiful!

As a matter of fact, when I die, I want to be buried at sea. Not my ashes, but my body. I will make those arrangements when the time comes, but if I don't or my demise is unexpected, you know my wish.

You have only one sibling, so learn to get along with her. She is not perfect and neither are you.

As you grow older and I have moved on to playing tennis in heaven, pull out this letter and read it again and again. I sincerely hope it brings you peace of mind and helps guide you through life's challenges.

I love you with all my heart and I cannot wait to see you again in heaven.

>   Love always,
>   Dad

ACKNOWLEDGMENTS

DENIAL: REFUSING TO ACKNOWLEDGE that something is wrong is a way of coping with stress, emotional conflict, and anxiety. Writing this book was a long and exhausting process, mainly because I didn't want to ever complete it. I searched night and day for meaningless tasks to do, all to avoid just sitting down and pouring out my emotions. Subconsciously, I convinced myself that by dragging the process out, I could somehow hold on to Nic and delay saying a final good-bye. The longer I procrastinated, the more vibrant his memories remained. *By delaying the book, I was still his dad.*

Through the help of some highly motivated, but loving friends, I accepted my denial and pushed forward with completing the book. Without them, I probably would still be dusting baseboards or polishing glasses I never use.

There are so many people to thank with helping me through my journey and encouraging me to finish the book. While I may not mention everyone, please know your kindness and prayers helped me through the most painful experience of my life. I know God placed you there for that purpose and I thank each and every one of you for all your efforts. Without you, there would be no *Dare to Ask God WHY?*

I wish to thank Arlene and Tiffany Williams for their enduring support and encouragement. The endless memories we shared as a family provided the foundation to writing this book. Thanks also to my extended family, Calvin and Deborah Williams, David and Pat Brown, Karrisa and Chelsea Brown, and Della Foster.

To all Nico's friends:

The love and care you showed us during our time of grief and afterwards is beyond words. We love you and thank God for you all. Gigi Avila, Gabby House, Sol Vilera-Ramos, Kylee Young, Corbin Ward, Clay Huddleston, Christina Noker, Kailey McKenzie, Lindsay Wilkerson, Shelby Black, Caitie Robertson, Ben Carpenter, Courtney Stansbury Johnson, Elise Watson, Kara Eichelkraut, Michael McKelva, Brennon, Collin Mulcahy, Stevo Frazee, Darshini Shah, Aaron Gonzales, Todd Loggins, Matt Mot, Sara Muldoon, Courtney Callaway, Katie Mahand Sherer, Lauren Kelly, Andres and Francisco Guerra, Oliver Chen, Jasmin Steele, Carolina Sommerstad, D'Andrea Ceasar, Colleen Gibson, Thomas Sizer, Alan Wilmot, Kara Ike, Becca Mott, Chelsea Morgan, Andre Arizpe, Rebekah Parker, Kade Johnston, Chelsea Bielitz, Adaeze Ejiogu, Shannon Curtis,

Kailey McKenzie, and Will Meador.

To the many people who played a pivotal role by being in the right place at the right time, I owe you so much. Thank you for giving me the little nudge I needed to keep going. Floyd and Deborah Leblanc, Aisha and Lenora Hunte, Torrey Boykin, Dwight "Stud" Boykins, Sarah Hinojosa, Anita Dewease, Patsy and Jamie Schanbaum, Anna Dragsbaek, Jason Sabo, Dr. Julie Boom, Rachel Cunningham, Dr. Carol Baker, Pastor Kirbyjon Caldwell, Dodie Osteen, Rep. Charlie Howard, Sen. Wendy Davis, Frankie Miley, Ashlee McClelland, Tina Montgomery, Reuben Joseph, Melanie Jackson, Seleta Bruton, Lesley Smith, and Thomas Britt.

To my best of friends who exhibited unwavering support when I thought there was no tomorrow. Thank you, Linda Kellough, Dr. Falanda Troutman, John Gray, and John Sudden.

A special thanks to Michelle Valdez who helped me understand that completing the book was just the beginning, and to Cynthia Stone at TREATY OAK PUBLISHERS who guided me through the treacherous waters of the publishing business.

Lastly, I thank God for trusting me to be obedient and providing me the resources to bring his message to fruition.

The NICO Williams Foundation

The NICO Williams Foundation is a nonprofit organization whose purpose is to bring awareness to Bacterial Meningitis, provide free vaccinations for the disease and to maintain a legacy for Nico. Presentations are available to educate parents and students about the dangers of Bacterial Meningitis.

For details, please visit:
nicowilliamsfoundation.org

All donations are tax deductible and are utilized for purposes consistent with the Foundation's tax exempt objectives. Every child dreams of their future possibilities and they deserve an opportunity to live out their dreams. With your help, The NICO Williams Foundation will provide that opportunity.

Remember: N.I.C.O.
Neglecting **I**mmunizations
Compromises **O**pportunity

ABOUT THE AUTHOR

Greg Williams is college administrator and a vaccination advocate. After his son died from bacterial meningitis in 2011, he worked with the 82nd Texas Legislature to modify the meningitis law that now includes all students and not just dorm residents. He spends his spare time lobbying at the state's capitol and educating the public about the deadly disease. He resides in the suburbs of Houston, Texas.

Greg Williams with his son Nic
photo courtesy of
Meningitis Angels

www.ingramcontent.com/pod-product-compliance
Lightning Source LLC
Chambersburg PA
CBHW071302110426
42743CB00042B/1144